U.S. Department of Justice
Office of Justice Programs
National Institute of Justice

I0476893

National Institute of Justice

Research Report

Electronic Crime Needs Assessment for State and Local Law Enforcement

U.S. Department of Justice
Office of Justice Programs
810 Seventh Street N.W.
Washington, DC 20531

Office of Justice Programs
World Wide Web Site
http://www.ojp.usdoj.gov

National Institute of Justice
World Wide Web Site
http://www.ojp.usdoj.gov/nij

Electronic Crime Needs Assessment for State and Local Law Enforcement

Hollis Stambaugh
David S. Beaupre
David J. Icove
Richard Baker
Wayne Cassaday
Wayne P. Williams

March 2001
NCJ 186276

Project Management Team

National Institute of Justice
Saralyn Borrowman
Amon Young

TriData Corporation
Hollis Stambaugh
Teresa Copping

U.S. Department of Justice
Wayne P. Williams (retired)

U.S. Department of State
David S. Beaupre

U.S. Navy Space and Naval Warfare Systems Center, Charleston, Security Department
Wayne Cassaday
Richard Baker

U.S. Tennessee Valley Authority Police
David J. Icove

This program was supported under award number 98–DT–R–076 to the Tennessee Valley Authority by the National Institute of Justice, Office of Justice Programs, U.S. Department of Justice. Findings and conclusions of the research reported here are those of the authors and do not necessarily reflect the official position or policies of the U.S. Department of Justice.

Preface

Just as the Industrial Revolution brought unprecedented opportunity two centuries ago, so too has the Information Age. But the astronomical rate at which global technology has grown has opened new windows of opportunity for crime as well as economic progress. In 1996, the U.S. Department of Justice said:

> Whether [technology] benefits us or injures us depends almost entirely on the fingers on the keyboard. So while the Information Age holds great promise, it falls, in part, upon law enforcement to ensure that users of networks do not become victims of New Age crime.[1]

The rapid proliferation of computer systems, telecommunications networks, and other related technologies that we rely on daily has created complex and far-reaching interdependencies as well as concomitant, widespread vulnerabilities.

Media reports of cyberthreats, whether perpetrated by hobbyist hackers, international terrorist organizations, or trusted employees, are increasing. According to a report released in 1998 by the Center for Strategic and International Studies:

> Almost all Fortune 500 corporations have been penetrated electronically by cybercriminals. The FBI estimates that electronic crimes are running at least $10 billion a year. But only 17 percent of the companies victimized report these intrusions to law enforcement agencies.[2]

In addition, a recent U.S. General Accounting Office report on computer threats cites:

> [T]he number of reported incidents handled by Carnegie-Mellon University's CERT [Computer Emergency Response Team] Coordination Center [a federally funded response team] has increased from 1,334 in 1993 to 4,398 during the first two quarters of 1999.[3]

Attacks against computer systems or networks are not new. One of the first highly publicized national electronic crime incidents occurred in November 1988. Then 23-year-old student Robert Morris launched a virus on the Internet. The "Morris Worm," as it later became known, caused parts of the Internet to collapse and drastically hampered electronic communications. Eventually, it infected more than 6,000 computers of the roughly 60,000 systems linked to the Internet at the time. Many corporations and government sites disconnected themselves from the Internet as news of the incident spread. Costs to repair the infected systems were estimated to be approximately $100 million. The temporary loss of confidence in the Internet extracted a cost that reached far beyond the direct monetary losses. Morris was sentenced to 3 years' probation and a $10,000 fine, a relatively light sentence compared with the penalties that would apply today.

In a current case, the Federal Bureau of Investigation (FBI) is investigating a gang that refers to itself as "Global Hell." The group is accused of hacking into the Web sites of the White House, the FBI, the U.S. Army, and the U.S. Department of the Interior, among others. At least two gang members have been convicted as a result of a nationwide law enforcement investigation targeting more than a dozen suspects. Thus far it appears as though Global Hell is more concerned with gaining notoriety for defacing prominent Web sites than with destroying or capturing sensitive information. Even so, Federal law enforcement officials had to spend hundreds of hours tracking down members of this gang. Investigating electronic crime is time consuming and costly—a problem most State and local investigators and computer forensic specialists are confronting. Any potential for growth in electronic crime raises serious concerns about the capability of law enforcement resources to keep pace.

In another high-profile case that attracted nation-wide attention, State and local law enforcement officers conducted an intense investigation and search for a suspect they believed created a malicious virus that spread worldwide. The search for the perpetrator of the "Melissa" virus involved five agencies and culminated in the arrest of a computer programmer in New Jersey in April 1999. The suspect faces charges of interruption of public communications, conspiracy, and theft of computer service—charges that carry a maximum penalty of 40 years in prison and a $480,000 fine. In this case, 7 search warrants and 11 communications data warrants were filed. In addition, the agency in charge of the investigation, the New Jersey State Police High Technology Crimes and Investigations Support Unit, coordinated with America Online, Inc., to obtain Internet account subscriber information and activity logs. The Melissa virus affected hundreds of thousands of computers in workplaces across the country. The total cost to repair these systems is estimated to be in the millions of dollars. This case highlights the responsibilities that State and local authorities have in national electronic crime cases such as these.

These examples give us a glimpse of the potential wave of electronic and online crime that could eventually affect most law enforcement agencies. Increasingly, our Nation's State and local law enforcement officers will be called on to detect information technology crime, analyze electronic evidence, and identify offenders. Most electronic crimes, such as the Morris Worm or those carried out by Global Hell, are not national security threats but wreak havoc nonetheless. Citizens are fleeced of millions of dollars, businesses suffer losses from online fraud, drug dealers and organized crime elements employ advanced encryption technology to evade law enforcement, pedophiles use the anonymity of cyberspace to stalk and molest children,

businesses increasingly are engaging in economic espionage, and cyberterrorists exploit vulnerabilities in our Nation's critical infrastructures.

The 1997 report of the President's Commission on Critical Infrastructure Protection sums up the urgency of the situation:

> We are convinced that our vulnerabilities are increasing steadily, that the means to exploit those weaknesses are readily available and that the costs associated with an effective attack continue to drop. What is more, the investments required to improve the situation—now still relatively modest—will rise if we procrastinate.[4]

As State and local law enforcement increasingly are relied on to protect us against these crimes, they need to be aware of what threats currently exist and, more important, be capable of handling present and emerging threats as they continue to arise.

Notes

1. White House, *International Crime Control Strategy*, Washington, DC: The White House, 1998: 68.

2. Center for Strategic and International Studies, Global Organized Crime Project, *Cybercrime . . . Cyberterrorism . . . Cyberwarfare . . . Averting an Electronic Waterloo*, Washington, DC: Center for Strategic and International Studies, 1998.

3. U.S. General Accounting Office, *Critical Infrastructure Protection: Comprehensive Strategy Can Draw on Year 2000 Experience*, doc. no. GAO/AIMD–00–1, Washington, DC: U.S. General Accounting Office, 1999: 8.

4. President's Commission on Critical Infrastructure Protection, *Critical Foundations: Protecting America's Infrastructures*, Washington, DC: President's Commission on Critical Infrastructure Protection, 1997: x.

Acknowledgments

The authors of this report extend their sincerest appreciation to the State and local representatives who took part in this study as well as to their agencies for allowing them to be a part of this important research project. Their contributions form the basis for this report, and we are grateful for their willingness to share their experiences and expertise in the field. We also acknowledge the valuable assistance provided by the four regional centers and the Border Research and Technology Center of the National Institute of Justice's (NIJ's) National Law Enforcement and Corrections Technology Center (NLECTC) system. The centers recommended law enforcement participants, scheduled visits, and served as hosts for the workshops. Special appreciation is extended to the following individuals:

NLECTC–Northeast (Northeastern Region), Rome, New York: John Ritz, Center Director; Fred Demma, Operations/Technical Assistance; and Robert DeCarlo, Jr., Operations/Technical Assistance.

NLECTC–Southeast (Southeastern Region), North Charleston, South Carolina: Tommy Sexton, Center Director; William Nettles, Deputy Director; William Deck, Law Enforcement Technologies; and Howard Alston, Research and Development.

NLECTC–Rocky Mountain (Rocky Mountain Region), Denver, Colorado: James Keller, Center Director; Karen Duffala, Director, Outreach Programs; and Courtney Klug, Assistant to the Director.

NLECTC–West (Western Region), El Segundo, California: Robert Pentz, Center Director; and Donald Buchwald, Computer Forensic Analyst.

Border Research and Technology Center, San Diego, California: Chris Aldridge, Center Director; and John Bott, Technical Director.

The authors recognize the Bureau of Justice Assistance and the National White Collar Crime Center (NW3C). In its capacity as the operations center for the National Cybercrime Training Partnership, NW3C spearheaded and funded a cybercrime training survey for State and local law enforcement agencies in 1997. That undertaking laid the foundation for and helped to shape the NIJ-sponsored assessment. Special appreciation is extended to the following individuals: Richard H. Ward III, Deputy Director, Bureau of Justice Assistance, U.S. Department of Justice; and Richard Johnston, Director, National White Collar Crime Center.

The authors also recognize the contributions made to this needs assessment effort by an advisory panel that was convened at the beginning of the project to assist with the formulation of the protocol. Members of the panel from NLECTC were Donald Buchwald, NLECTC–West; William Deck, NLECTC–Southeast; Fred Demma, NLECTC–Northeast, and Karen Duffala, NLECTC–Rocky Mountain. Other members included Dean Chatfield, NW3C; Barry Leese, Maryland State Police; Steve Ronco, Hi-Tech Crimes Unit, San Jose Police Department; Daniel Ryan, Science Applications International Corporation; Gail Thackeray, Maricopa County, Arizona, Attorney's Office; and Dick Johnston, NW3C.

Contents

Exhibits

Executive Summary

Not long ago, the incidence of crimes that involved computers or electronic media was negligible. Currently, State and local law enforcement agencies routinely encounter evidence of electronic crimes, including online fraud, child pornography, embezzlement, economic espionage, and cyberstalking. Law enforcement also encounters crimes classified as cyberterrorism. These incidents have included attempts to penetrate electronic systems that control critical infrastructures. The task of investigating and prosecuting electronic crimes and cyberterrorism is complicated by the anonymity afforded perpetrators through the Internet, by a "borderless" environment, and by the variables in State and foreign laws.

To address this growing problem, the National Institute of Justice (NIJ), in conjunction with the National Cybercrime Training Partnership—a high-technology training consortium led by the Computer Crime and Intellectual Property Section of the U.S. Department of Justice—initiated a national study in fall 1998 to assess the needs of State and local law enforcement agencies to combat electronic crime and cyberterrorism. Another objective of the study was to develop a better understanding of the various aspects of electronic crime, such as the most prevalent targets, offenders, and motives behind this type of crime.

NIJ established a project management team to oversee all aspects of the study. The team tasked the four regional facilities and the Border Research and Technology Center of NIJ's National Law Enforcement and Corrections Technology Center (NLECTC) system to identify leading law enforcement representatives in the electronic crime field. Ultimately, 126 individuals representing 114 agencies participated in the study. Collectively, they represented a variety of urban and rural jurisdictions and a diverse selection of agencies that included State police, city police, State bureaus of investigation, sheriff's departments, crime laboratories, and regulatory offices. The participants were asked to

consider six specific topic areas in providing their input about what is needed to combat electronic crime:

- State and local perspectives on electronic crime.
- Profile of types of electronic crimes and investigation needs.
- System vulnerability, critical infrastructure, and cyberterrorism.
- Forensic evidence collection and analysis.
- Legal issues and prosecution.
- Training.

The project team analyzed the participants' input and documented the findings in a draft report. The project team assembled a group of subject matter experts in the field of electronic crime to review and comment on the draft.

The Critical Ten

Today's technological advancements occur with such frequency that keeping up to date on the latest electronic-based systems and their associated technologies (the new "weapons" of criminals) poses a daunting task for State and local law enforcement agencies with limited resources and personnel. Criminals operating in cyberspace continuously employ new techniques and methods, thereby making it more difficult for law enforcement to keep pace. Notwithstanding state-of-the-art changes, the critical State and local law enforcement needs mentioned in this report are not likely to change in the near future. Although the participants identified more than 100 needs and issues that require attention to keep pace with the rapid escalation of computer crime, the most frequently voiced concerns are grouped into the "Critical Ten" in this report (chapter 4). A brief synopsis of the Critical Ten needs identified by the study's participants follows.

Critical need 1: Public awareness

A solid information and awareness program is needed to educate the general public, elected and appointed officials, and the private sector about the incidence and impact of electronic crimes. Most individuals are unaware of the extent to which their lives, financial status, businesses, families, or privacy might be affected by electronic crime. Nor are they aware of how quickly the threat is growing. Unless the public is informed of the increase in crimes committed using the Internet, cybercriminals will continue to steal people's money, personal identities, and property.

Critical need 2: Data and reporting

More comprehensive data are needed to understand the extent and impact of electronic crime. Without more complete data on incidents, offenders, forensic problems, and case outcomes, it will be difficult to track regional or national trends in electronic crime.

Critical need 3: Uniform training and certification courses

Law enforcement officers and forensic scientists need specific levels of training and certification to carry out their respective duties when investigating electronic crimes, collecting and examining evidence, and providing courtroom testimony. Participants were adamant that this training should reflect State and local priorities. Prosecutors, judges, probation and parole officers, and defense attorneys need basic training in electronic crime.

Critical need 4: Onsite management assistance for electronic crime units and task forces

State and local law enforcement agencies need assistance in developing computer investigation units, creating collaborative computer forensics capabilities, organizing task forces, and establishing programs with private industry. Law enforcement personnel are seeking assistance about best practices and lessons learned from existing, successful investigation units. Likewise, many of the agencies called for a county or regional task force approach to the technically challenging and time-consuming job of investigating crimes involving electronic evidence.

Critical need 5: Updated laws

Effective, uniform laws and regulations that keep pace with electronic crime need to be applied on the Federal and State levels. New technology developed for legitimate uses quickly can become a tool for the commission of a crime. As a result, the criminal justice system needs to stay abreast of state-of-the-art methods used to carry out these new types of crimes. Also, the disparity in penal codes among States impedes interstate pursuit of offenders, among other complications.

Critical need 6: Cooperation with the high-tech industry

Increased cooperation between industry and government provides the best opportunity to control electronic crime and protect the Nation's critical infrastructure. Private industry can assist by reporting incidents of electronic crime committed against their systems, helping to sponsor training, joining task forces, and sharing equipment for examining electronic evidence. Crime solvers need industry's full support and cooperation to control electronic crime.

Critical need 7: Special research and publications

Investigators, forensic laboratory specialists, and prosecutors need a comprehensive directory of training and other resources to help them combat electronic crime. State and local law enforcement agencies also are asking for a "Yellow Pages" of national and State experts and resources. A "who's who" of electronic crime investigators, unit managers, prosecutors, laboratory technicians, equipment manufacturers, expert witnesses, and so forth would be a well-received guidebook for many practitioners who frequently noted the need for information on how to contact their colleagues in other communities.

Critical need 8: Management awareness and support

Many participants and facilitators expressed concern that senior managers do not fully understand the impact of electronic crime and the level of expertise and tools needed to investigate and prepare successful cases for prosecution. Of the police chiefs and managers who are willing to support an investigative capability for electronic crime, they often must do so at the expense of other units or assign dual investigation responsibilities to personnel.

Critical need 9: Investigative and forensic tools

There is a significant and immediate need for up-to-date technological tools and equipment for State and local law enforcement agencies to conduct electronic crime investigations. Most electronic crime cases cannot be thoroughly investigated and developed without the benefit of higher end computer technology, which is beyond the budgets of many law enforcement agencies.

Critical need 10: Structuring a computer crime unit

As communities begin to address electronic crime, they grapple with how best to structure a computer (or electronic) crime unit that will both investigate crimes involving computers and analyze electronic evidence. The experts are divided over whether and how the duties of investigation and forensic analysis should be divided. State and local law enforcement agencies suggested that new research be conducted to identify the key staffing requirement issues for computer crime units.

Conclusion

Whether the need is high-end computer forensic training or onsite task force development assistance, progress needs to be accomplished quickly and in a coordinated manner. The sophistication of technology used by offenders is increasing at a pace that significantly taxes the resources of the public sector at the State and local levels. This report, which identifies the needs of State and local law enforcement agencies to combat electronic crime, should serve as an impetus for creating timely initiatives that address these needs. Both immediate action and future study are essential.

Introduction

Background

On January 10, 1998, the National Cybercrime Training Partnership (NCTP), formerly known as the Infotech Training Working Group, issued a summary report of focus group meetings with 31 chiefs of police held in San Francisco, California, and Charleston, South Carolina.[1] The report was prepared under the direction of Wayne P. Williams, then Senior Litigation Counsel for the U.S. Department of Justice, Criminal Division, Computer Crime and Intellectual Property Section.

The purpose of the NCTP focus group meetings was to elicit from participants the status of computer and high-technology crime and identify what training and technical assistance would be of greatest value to State and local law enforcement agencies. The 31 representatives covered a training base of 84,000 persons. The Bureau of Justice Assistance, an agency of the U.S. Department of Justice, sponsored these meetings.

The following key issues were raised during the sessions:

- Awareness of the computer and high-technology crime problem among managers, the public, and politicians is low.

- All participants endorsed the NCTP goals of creating and maintaining a knowledge base of critical information, supporting research and development of cybertools for law enforcement, and providing training with "train the trainer" assistance.

- The demand for electronic crime-related training exceeds the availability of current courses.

- A strong demand exists for nontraditional training modalities, which include mobile training teams, CD–ROM-based training, and distance learning.

- Due to tight budgets, the demand for cost-effective training has increased.

- Technical assistance is required in establishing computer crime units and task forces.

- There is a strong need for interconnectivity among laboratories to coordinate the analysis of computer evidence.

NCTP continues to play a leadership role in national cybercrime training initiatives and works at all levels of law enforcement to develop long-range strategies, raise public awareness of the problem, and focus the momentum on numerous efforts.

In an effort to broaden the scope of information on electronic crime needs, NIJ initiated a wider study, designed to augment the NCTP survey while both expanding the number of participants and the topic areas covered. NIJ wanted to hear from a range of law enforcement agencies about their experiences to date with electronic crime incidents and how they are positioned to investigate, handle evidence from, and prosecute this type of crime. NIJ created a management team (see "Project Management Team") to oversee the project and prepare findings.

Project Management Team

National Institute of Justice
Saralyn Borrowman
Amon Young

TriData Corporation
Hollis Stambaugh
Teresa Copping

U.S. Department of Justice
Wayne P. Williams (retired)

U.S. Department of State
David S. Beaupre

U.S. Navy Space and Naval Warfare Systems Center, Charleston, Security Department
Wayne Cassaday
Richard Baker

U.S. Tennessee Valley Authority Police
David J. Icove

This report presents the information about how the study was structured. It also documents what State and local law enforcement officials told the team about their experiences with electronic crime. Finally, the report comments on the implications of the research results and offers suggestions for future endeavors.

Study Challenges

The two early challenges for the research were how to define electronic crime and how to present cyberterrorism in the context of State and local experience. There was consensus among the project team members that the issue of systems vulnerability, from the standpoint of critical infrastructure protection, would be included under cyberterrorism. Even though Federal law enforcement agencies have the leading role in a cyberterrorist incident, State and local law enforcement agencies will need to be increasingly vigilant and prepared to handle critical infrastructure protection issues because they are the first responders.

The complexities involved in tracking a potential cyberterrorist incident, discovering the point of entry, and resolving cross-jurisdictional issues make it difficult for many State and local law enforcement agencies to identify when a cyberterrorist incident has taken place. In most cases, it is not immediately clear whether an intrusion is being perpetrated by a local recreational hacker impressing a friend with his skills, a cyberterrorist trying to disrupt the Nation's air traffic control systems, or a foreign intelligence service accessing sensitive classified government information. These scenarios can happen, and law enforcement will have to be prepared to deal with them when they occur.

To ensure continuity throughout the assessment, definitions of electronic crime were developed to provide a baseline for the research. They also provided a point of reference throughout the workshops. Because crimes committed against and with computers and information systems can be defined and categorized in many ways, there currently exists no universally accepted definitions of electronic crime and cyberterrorism. The definitions compiled for this study are derived from various sources and reflect widely accepted terminology at this time. The management team agreed on the following definitions:

- **Electronic crime.** Crimes including but not limited to fraud, theft, forgery, child pornography or exploitation, stalking, traditional white-collar crimes, privacy violations, illegal drug transactions, espionage, computer intrusions, or any other offenses that occur in an electronic environment for the express purpose of economic gain or with the intent to destroy or otherwise inflict harm on another person or institution. (This definition was compiled from various sources.)

- **Cyberterrorism (or information systems terrorism).** The premeditated, politically motivated attack against information systems, computer programs, and data to deny service or acquire information with the intent to disrupt the political, social, or physical infrastructure of a target, resulting in violence against the public. The attacks are perpetrated by subnational groups or clandestine agents who use information warfare tactics to achieve the traditional terrorist goals and objectives of engendering public fear and disorientation through disruption of services and random or massive destruction of life or property.[2]

Organization of the Report

This report contains four major chapters: This chapter places into context the format and purpose of the report. Chapter 2 summarizes the methodology employed by the management team for the study. Chapter 3 outlines the study's findings by the six subject areas along with an analysis of the results. Chapter 4 comments on the top 10 needs identified through the study and what the data may indicate are gaps in State and local resources; suggestions are presented as to how those needs could be met. After a series of reviews by the management team, the facilitators, and the subject matter experts who reviewed the draft, several recurring themes emerged. Those themes form the basis for the report's conclusions. The report includes three appendixes—a list of the participants by State, a glossary of terms and acronyms, and contact information for each of the report contributors.

The State and local participants were invited to express their views openly. A rule of nonattribution was established and honored because the team wanted participants to voice their opinions without constraint. Many insightful statements were made during the workshops. These quotes are included in chapter 3 to support the findings; however, they are presented without reference to the particular speaker.

Notes

1. Williams, W.P., T.A. Bresnick, and D.M. Buede, *Summary Report of Focus Groups,* Washington, DC: U.S. Department of Justice, Criminal Division, Computer Crime and Intellectual Property Section, National Cybercrime Training Partnership, 1998.

2. Pollitt, Mark M., 1997, "Cyberterrorism: Fact or Fancy?" Proceedings of the 20th National Information Systems Security Conference, Baltimore.

Research Methodology

Overview

This research initiative employed individual sessions and workshop groups composed of State and local law enforcement officers and other criminal justice officials who are directly involved in handling electronic crimes. The National Institute of Justice's (NIJ's) major instruction to the project team was to ensure that the study covered a broad and representative sample of participants, agencies, and geographic regions. This was achieved by selecting participants from all 50 States who had experience in dealing with electronic crimes and who represented a broad base of agencies from urban to more rural jurisdictions.

The four regional facilities and the Border Research and Technology Center of NIJ's National Law Enforcement and Corrections Technology Center (NLECTC) system helped identify candidates for inclusion in the study. They also hosted the meetings where the research was conducted and identified participants for consideration. The use of the centers was logical because of their diverse geographic representations for law enforcement, their direct relationship with NIJ, and their potential

future roles in the delivery of technical and training assistance. Moreover, the centers had been involved in a previous inventory by NIJ that collected information on local and State technology needs to combat terrorism.[1]

Exhibit 1 shows the geographic distribution of the NLECTC system.

Validity, Reliability, and Expertise

The management team met in fall 1998 to develop and implement the new study. The team outlined the tasks necessary to accomplish this work and established a project timeline. Early deliberations revolved around the means to ensure:

- Validity of the study results.
- Reliability of the data.
- Broad expert input into all phases of the project.

The team implemented several steps to address validity and reliability measures. The team established criteria to identify State and local law enforcement representatives with knowledge of and

---

Exhibit 1. The NLECTC System

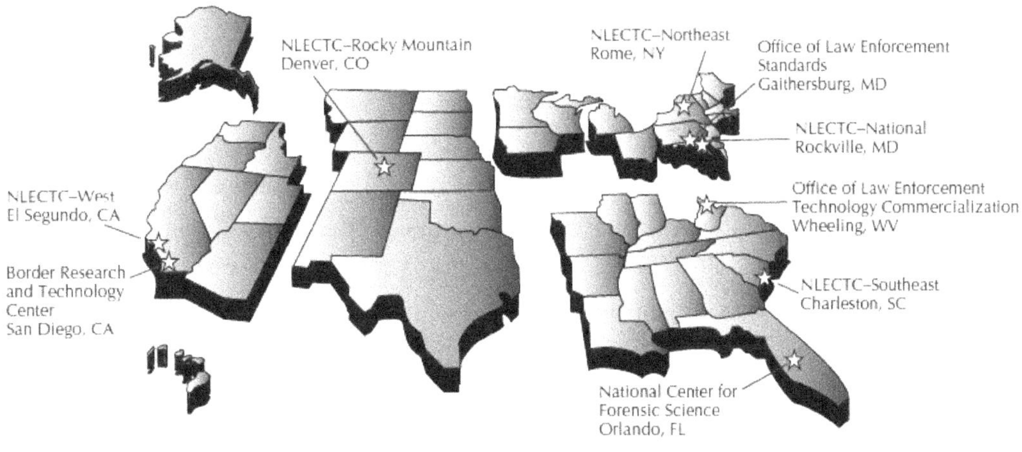

NLECTC–Rocky Mountain
Denver, CO

NLECTC–Northeast
Rome, NY

Office of Law Enforcement Standards
Gaithersburg, MD

NLECTC–National
Rockville, MD

NLECTC–West
El Segundo, CA

Office of Law Enforcement Technology Commercialization
Wheeling, WV

Border Research and Technology Center
San Diego, CA

NLECTC–Southeast
Charleston, SC

National Center for Forensic Science
Orlando, FL

responsibility for electronic crime investigations and enforcement to be study participants. The criteria was applied to screen referrals from NIJ's National Law Enforcement and Technology Center system, management team members, and leads obtained through a literature review.

In addition to assigning specific criteria for State and local representatives, the team sought representation from all 50 States. The team was careful to accommodate a reasonable balance among the types and sizes of jurisdictions represented, although an absolute representative sample was not attempted. Indeed, there are many more small towns and cities than there are metropolitan areas. However, the electronic crime caseloads of a community with a population of 40,000 are generally not sufficient to warrant a special electronic crime unit, and the study needed information from law enforcement agencies with some level of experience in investigating and prosecuting electronic crime. Thus, although smaller jurisdictions are critical to this report, to have had them represented proportionate to their numbers would have netted less data about incidents.

The team took additional steps to enhance the reliability and validity of study results. For example, a profile listing the required experience and skills was used to identify and select the facilitators—those individuals assigned to conduct the workshops. The facilitators attended a daylong training session at TriData Corporation in Arlington, Virginia, to prepare for the field work. The training was intended to strengthen interfacilitator reliability and establish uniform procedures for managing the workshops,

documenting the data, defining specific electronic crime issues, and handling questions uniformly in the process of collecting information.

The management team also sought the benefit of many experts in the field to guide both the design and the implementation of the study. Early in the process, the team established a national advisory panel. The panel and the management team met at TriData to review the project's goals and debate which issues and questions about electronic crime were most appropriate for the field work with State and local law enforcement agency representatives. These deliberations resulted in a study protocol that became the operational blueprint for the workshops. Advisory panel members included representatives from the NLECTC system, State and local police agencies, the National White Collar Crime Center, private industry, and a county attorney's office.

After the workshops were completed, TriData processed and analyzed the information and wrote a preliminary draft report. From that report, a draft project report was produced. The team assembled a group of experts on electronic crime to provide advice and comments (see "Subject Matter Experts"). These subject matter experts met with the management team in Knoxville to dissect the findings, review the first draft of the report, and offer constructive criticism.

Selection Criteria

As previously mentioned, steps were taken to ensure that selected agencies and their representatives

---

Subject Matter Experts

Frank S. Cilluffo	Center for Strategic and International Studies, Washington, D.C.
Al Evans	Maryland State Police, Columbia, Maryland
James H. Fetzer III	U.S. Tennessee Valley Authority Police, Knoxville, Tennessee
Mary R. Holt	Alabama Department of Forensic Sciences, Birmingham, Alabama
Stephen D. McFall	Federal Bureau of Investigation, Knoxville, Tennessee
Howard Schmidt	Microsoft Corporation, Redmond, Washington
Raemarie Schmidt	National White Collar Crime Center, Fairmont, West Virginia
William Tafoya	Governors State University, University Park, Illinois
David Vanzant	FBI Academy, Quantico, Virginia
Wayne P. Williams	U.S. Department of Justice, Washington, D.C. (retired)

encompassed a range of jurisdiction types (cities, counties, and metropolitan areas) and law enforcement functions (investigators, unit commanders, State police, district attorneys, forensics examiners, etc.). All the participants have responsibility for electronic crime in their respective agencies; most have served in the computer crime unit or forensic laboratory as an investigator or manager.

A total of 126 individuals representing 114 agencies participated in this effort. Exhibit 2 depicts the number of participants by NLECTC center location; a complete list of participants, grouped by State, is provided in appendix A.

Participants also were selected based on their experience, and a mix of investigators, chiefs, captains, sergeants, prosecutors, and others was achieved. Exhibit 3 profiles the participants by title.

Facilitators

At the beginning of the project, the management team developed a list of qualifications for selecting

the project's facilitators, including expertise in electronic crime issues and strong interpersonal skills. Facilitators also were required to commit at least 2 weeks to the project. Based on the requirements, several highly qualified candidates were recommended by members of the advisory panel, NLECTC representatives, and the management team. The management team met in Washington, D.C., to discuss the candidates. After careful consideration, consensus was reached, and seven facilitators were selected from the pool of candidates. The facilitators, representing various backgrounds in law enforcement, intelligence, and academia, were chosen based on their particular professional experience and proven track record for facilitating meetings and focus group sessions (see "Facilitators").

Once selected, the candidates were hired as consultants to the project. They were sent background material and a letter informing them of their obligation to attend a daylong training session at TriData Corporation. A professional facilitator was hired by TriData to conduct the training. The training was

Exhibit 2. Number of Participants, by NLECTC Center

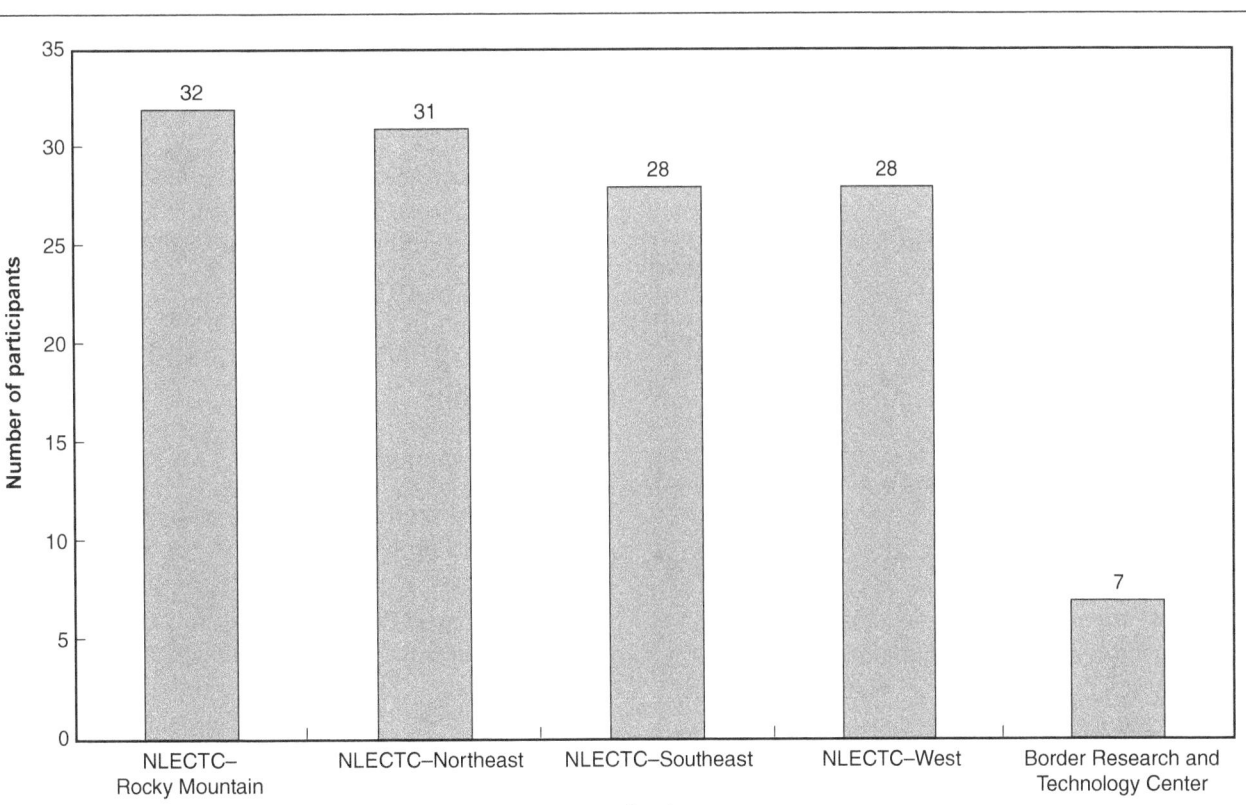

Exhibit 3. Profile of Participants, by Title

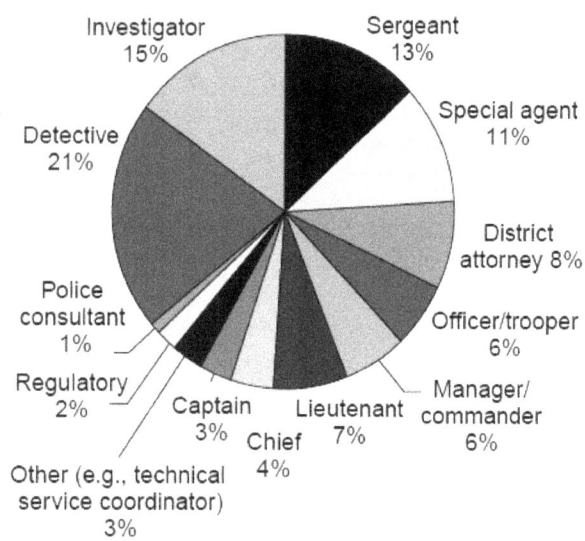

Note: Values are rounded to the nearest number.

Facilitators

Ross Ashley
ISX Corporation

Kathleen Barch
Ohio Attorney General's Office

James Cannady
Georgia Institute of Technology

Thomas Kennedy
Center for Technology Commercialization

Barry Leese
Maryland State Police

Dan Mares
Mares and Company, LLC

G. Thomas Steele
Maryland State Police

---

geared toward assuring that the assessment instrument—or protocol, which facilitators used to elicit information from participants—would be uniformly administered during the four site visits (Southeastern Region, March 2–4, 1999; Western Region/Border Research and Technology Center, March 9–11, 1999; Rocky Mountain Region, March 23–25,

1999; and Northeastern Region, March 23–25, 1999). The facilitators were briefed on the project objectives, the operative definitions, and the design of the assessment protocol. They were also provided with a common outline to capture information in the field and were given the opportunity to practice interviewing one another. This allowed them to become familiar with the assessment instrument and comfortable with the interviewing technique.

Afterward, the facilitators participated in a mock workshop in which they were subjected to intentional disruptions by the trainer that simulated potential field scenarios. The trainer gauged their responses and provided feedback on how they should handle each particular scenario. This portion of the training provided the facilitators with "lessons learned" and an opportunity to work with the assessment instrument in a hands-on, live setting.

At least two facilitators attended each of the four site visits. One facilitator led the group discussion; the other took detailed notes. In some cases, a third facilitator assisted the notetaker or conducted interviews. After each session, the facilitators compared notes to ensure that the information they gathered was accurate. When the site visits were complete, the facilitators submitted a summary of their observations and analysis of the information captured in the field. These summaries assisted in the formulation of the report findings and the "Critical Ten" needs outlined in chapter 4. In addition, three facilitators met in Washington, D.C., to debrief the management team on the most salient points gathered in the field.

Structuring the Interviews and Group Discussions

Literature review

Work on this project began with an extensive literature review. Journal articles, speeches and testimony, seminar reports, and newspaper articles were collected from Internet searches. Several advisory panel members recommended books and papers on electronic crime, cyberterrorism, and information warfare to review. Researchers kept abreast of topical seminars and reports from those proceedings as well. This research guided the development of the assessment instrument. Moreover, the literature review provided insight into how the study should define the role of computers in electronic crime. For the purposes of this study, computer-related crime was defined using three parameters:

- A computer can be used as a *weapon*—a means for perpetrating crimes. Computers can be used to attack another computer to acquire stored information, deny service, or damage a system. Computers can also be used to manufacture currency, certified checks, credit cards, and insurance cards and policies. They also can facilitate the acquisition of new identity information such as passports or birth certificates. Computers can be used in support of terrorist trade craft; that is, by using the Internet as a means to disseminate terrorist propaganda, recruit others, or engage in fundraising activities. Intelligence gathering or economic espionage conducted by foreign intelligence services, terrorist organizations, hate groups, and others also is a concern. These groups can probe the Internet for open source information or employ hacking techniques to gain access to sensitive proprietary data from the private sector or classified government systems.

- A computer as a *target* involves the computer as the actual object of an offense. Information contained on a system can be manipulated, stolen, or compromised for fraudulent and other criminal purposes. A hacker can gain unauthorized access and remove, alter, or destroy information or engage in a denial-of-service attack against a system. For example, the target of an attack could be a 911 center or a computer-aided dispatch service in which the system is flooded with calls, causing it to crash and be rendered inoperable. Infrastructure systems are vulnerable to attack because many rely on public switch telecommunications and are interdependent. In many cases, a single-point failure from an attack results in more than one system being victimized.

- A computer can be a *corollary* to an offense as a storage medium—an electronic filing cabinet—of potential evidentiary information. Individuals can use a computer to store tools, information, or files. Child pornography, financial ledgers used by drug dealers, potential terrorist target lists and attack plans, and other illicit activity can be stored on computers, thereby becoming receptacles of evidence.

Protocol development

The assessment instrument was developed over a period of several months by the project team members. It was based on the combined institutional knowledge of law enforcement officers, prosecutors, researchers, and technologists. The advisory panel, which included academia, industry, and Federal Government representatives, also contributed. The protocol went through numerous critiques and several reviews before it was used in the field. In addition to the advisory panel members, the protocol was reviewed by State and local law enforcement representatives knowledgeable in electronic crime to further enhance its substance and credibility within the State and local law enforcement community.

The protocol ensured that the discussions remained structured, in both individual and workshop settings. "Summary of Workshop Protocol Topics" outlines the six major topics and their purposes.

Workshop procedures

At the workshops, the facilitators introduced each section by clarifying the purpose of the topic. For example, the participants were told that the first section, State and local perspectives on electronic crime, was intended to "provide background information on your understanding, responsibilities, involvement, training, and agency experience in dealing with electronic crime." The design of each discussion item within the individual sections ensured that a logical progression of responses took place. The facilitators worked in pairs to direct the workshops and individually for the one-on-one meetings.

Two types of sessions were held; the same issues were discussed in both formats:

- Individual meetings, lasting approximately 1^1/$_2$ hours.

- Workshops generally involving three to six participants from different agencies, lasting approximately 3 hours.

Management of field work

Performance in the field was closely managed. One or more members of the management team was present to help conduct the workshops and

Summary of Workshop Protocol Topics

State and local perspectives on electronic crime: Obtain background information on the understanding, responsibilities, involvement, training, and agency experience in dealing with electronic crime.

Profile of types of electronic crimes and investigation needs: Document agency readiness to respond to these events and to obtain feedback on what obstacles might hinder these investigations.

System vulnerability, critical infrastructure, and cyberterrorism: Determine the vulnerabilities of local public safety agencies' systems and the incidence of attacks against critical infrastructures.

Forensic evidence collection and analysis: Determine agency preparedness for identification and proper collection of forensic evidence.

Legal issues and prosecution: Assess agency awareness concerning legal issues surrounding electronic crime as well as what resources are needed to handle electronic crime cases in court.

Training: Review the availability of electronic crime-related training and specify the unmet training needs.

assist the facilitators. As questions concerning the project arose, team members provided insight into the rationale behind the questions under discussion and guided the workshops accordingly. In addition, a representative from each NLECTC facility also was available to handle other situations (e.g., logistics, setting up conference facilities). This allowed a member of the management team to closely monitor operations, provide constant feedback at each site,

introduce the purpose and background of the project at the beginning of each session, and ensure continuity throughout the workshops.

Note

1. National Institute of Justice, *Inventory of State and Local Law Enforcement Technology Needs to Combat Terrorism,* Research in Brief, Washington, DC: U.S. Department of Justice, National Institute of Justice, January 1999, NCJ 173384.

Findings

State and Local Perspectives on Electronic Crime

The researchers sought information from participants about their experiences with electronic crime cases as well as their individual responsibilities, training, and level of management support in handling computer crimes. Discussions focused on trends in electronic crime caseloads, awareness and support from upper management, and the priority level given to investigating and prosecuting electronic crime cases. A key discussion point in this section concerns profiling the most common targets and offenders.

Trends in caseload and priority status

More than 80 percent of the participants noted a measurable increase in computer and electronic crimes reported to and investigated by their agencies—in particular, traditional crimes such as fraud and theft committed using computers and unlawful activity committed via the Internet. The increase in reporting, they commented, is due to increased awareness of computer-related crime and a higher incidence of these crimes. A small minority of State and local representatives stated there was no change, and a few did not know. According to the 1999 Computer Security Institute/Federal Bureau of Investigation (CSI/FBI) survey of 521 security professionals in U.S. corporations, government agencies, financial institutions, and universities, the number of people reporting electronic crime to law enforcement has dramatically increased. Thirty-two percent of the CSI/FBI survey respondents reported electronic crimes to law enforcement, an increase over the prior 3 years in which only 17 percent reported these crimes to law enforcement.[1] Although this increase is significant, corporations and citizens are generally reluctant to report these crimes to law enforcement for a variety of reasons.

"There has been a definite noticeable shift in the priority of [electronic] crime. It is far more media sensitive than ever."

The investigative priority for electronic crimes may not be keeping pace with the growth in caseload, according to the assessment results. Ninety-five out of 123 participants who responded (77 percent) to the survey discussed in this Research Report said electronic crime cases are assigned a low to medium priority within their agency. The one exception to this rule is with cases related to child pornography and child exploitation, which often are given high priority. The low priority given to cases overall can be explained, at least in part, by the problems associated with accurately depicting the crime (see exhibit 4).

"They [management] are very aware that they are unaware. They know the problem [electronic crime] exists but don't know what to do about it."

"Child pornography cases get a high priority, even though generally all electronic crime gets a medium to low priority in the agency."

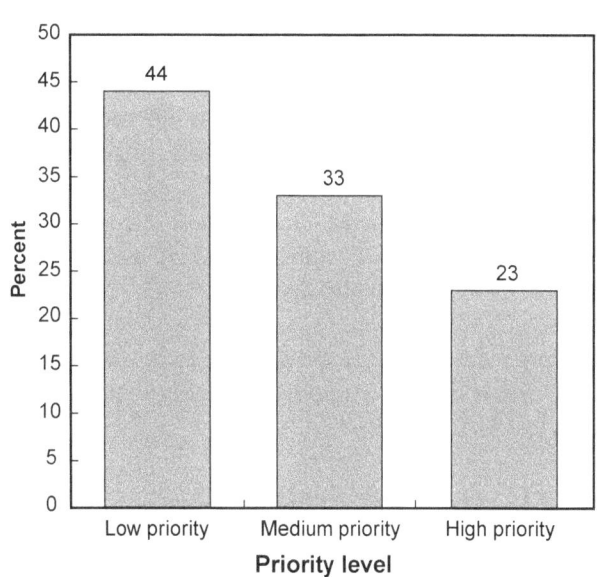

Exhibit 4. Investigative Priority of Electronic Crime Cases

Note: 124 of 126 par icipants responded.

"This field needs to be validated to the same level as homicide."

Electronic crime units

Half of the agencies involved in the study (62 of 124) have a formal electronic crime unit within the agency. The unit is responsible for all special electronic crime investigations. In some communities, the "unit" consists of only one investigator. In others, several investigators work electronic crime cases and evidence and prepare the cases for prosecution. Most jurisdictions without this type of unit believe it would be important to establish one in the near future.

"We need to build a team that handles forensic evidence."

"Electronic crime is handled as part of the specific crime of which it is a part, e.g., fraud unit, vice unit, narcotics unit. The command officer in each of these handles the electronic crime component. We need a unit dedicated to computer crime."

"We don't let a drug crime unit break down a homicide site, why will we let them break down a computer crime scene?"

Interagency electronic crime task forces

Only about one-third of the study participants reported that their agency is a member of a Federal, State, or local interagency electronic crime task force. For purposes of this study, the concept of a task force was defined in broad terms to include formal operational task forces in which two or more law enforcement agencies participate in a regional, State, or Federal task force configuration. Policy and advisory task forces were not included. Only those that included a law enforcement entity were considered, and both forensic and investigative task forces were covered.

"Regional task forces are the way to go. You have to bring in experts and have them help out the smaller jurisdictions."

"You're not going to make the average police department capable of dealing with a cybercrime; it's something that's so technical and so fluid that

only regional or Federal task forces will be able to deal with electronic crime on an effective level."

The study data show there is a significant regional difference in task force involvement. Electronic crime task forces are far more common in the Western region (see exhibit 1, chapter 2) than in any other part of the country. More than half of the task forces identified through the assessment are located in Arizona, California, Nevada, Oregon, Texas, and Washington. One possible explanation for this high representation of task forces is that many Silicon Valley companies have a strong, vested interest in enhancing State and local investigations and forensic capabilities. Cooperation between the private and public sectors was more frequently cited by participants from this geographic area as well. Exhibit 5 shows the breakdown of task force participation by region.

Reporting electronic crime

The vast majority of respondents expressed concern about the underreporting of computer crimes, notably in the private sector. Although caseloads are increasing in all parts of the country, computer crime investigators believe that is only the tip of the iceberg. A common complaint is that there is a large number of unreported cases occurring in the private

Exhibit 5. Percentage of Participants Involved in Task Forces, by Region

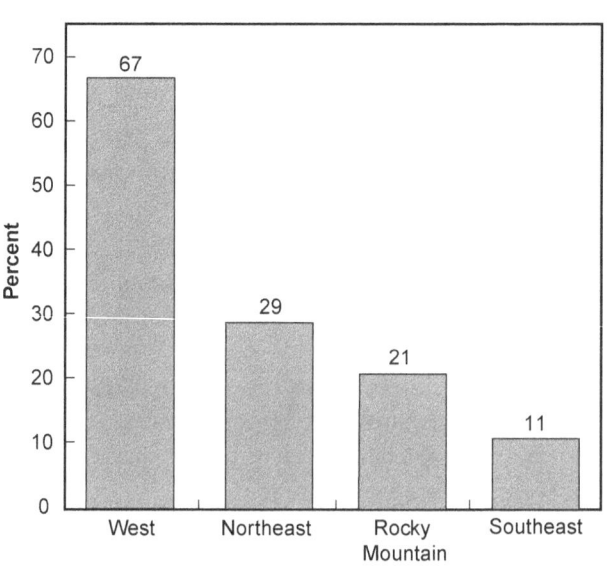

sector, especially the major information technology and banking industries. Indeed, although few private-sector cases are reported, the 1999 CSI/FBI survey revealed that 62 percent of respondents experienced computer security breaches.[2]

"Underreporting of these types of crimes is a serious problem, one that makes it almost impossible to validate this crime as a major problem."

Prosecution

When electronic crimes are reported to law enforcement agencies, the cases tend to be accepted for adjudication. Like other types of cases, an electronic crime case must meet basic criteria governing the alleged offender, the evidence chain of custody, and the quality of the investigation. For cases that do not go forward, the participants enumerated the reasons why. For example, 21 of the respondents said some of their cases get stalled because there is insufficient evidence to prove the crime was committed or the guilty party was responsible. Others (34) identified one or more of the following problems:

- Insufficient prosecutor knowledge and experience.
- Electronic crime cases not a priority.
- Lack of judicial interest in electronic crime cases.
- Lack of responding officer training.
- Lack of cooperation in extradition requests.

Many opinions were expressed about the status of electronic crime within the criminal justice system. A representative from the Southeast had encountered the attitude, "There are so many other cases to deal with that are more important." Several of the participants who met with project facilitators during the Western Region sessions commented about the lack of forensic expertise and expert witnesses, how agencies are overwhelmed by research requirements and the lack of data mining, and how pursuing electronic crime cases is costly. Concern also was expressed about incidents in which untrained officers inadvertently had tampered with the evidence.

The Rocky Mountain Region's series of meetings also drew several comments. Participants noted that poor computer crime laws stipulate that computer crimes can be processed only as a parallel crime to a charge that carries a greater penalty. According to

several individuals, the necessary manpower and resources are not available to prosecute electronic crimes. "Prosecutors like traditional crimes, not data trails," mentioned another official.

During the Northeastern Region workshops, some prosecution roadblocks that were mentioned included:

- The complainant (victim) does not want to prosecute.
- The amount of time to prepare a case is too great.
- There is a lack of resources to track offenders.
- Cooperation among law enforcement, district attorneys, and judges is poor.

Targets of electronic crime

There were excellent discussions at all the sites concerning the most frequent targets of electronic crime. The participants were asked to prioritize their choices in terms of the three most frequent targets. In many instances, a particular target is the "victim"—the ultimate goal of the offender. However, several layers of "targets" between the first and the last entry and exit points are used as launch pads and intermediaries to attack yet a different target. The interdependency of most systems is linked directly to the complexities in classifying victims of electronic attack.

A hypothetical example to illustrate this point is a telecommunications system that is attacked in Florida. A hacker or cyberterrorist breaks into and steals a student's account at the University of California and uses that account to conduct the hack into the telecommunications system in Florida. The hacker, however, is located in Sweden. Although the telecommunications system is the intended victim, the student's computer in California was exploited and used as a launch pad to mask the intrusion in Florida, making it harder for authorities to trace where the attack originated.

For this assessment, participants were asked to state the most frequent targets from their experiences in dealing with electronic crimes, regardless of launch pad or exit and entry scenarios. Overall, participants ranked businesses, individuals, and financial institutions as the first, second, and third most frequent targets, respectively. Exhibit 6 depicts the overall results.

Electronic crime offenders

In addition to determining the most frequent targets, the researchers also were interested in determining, from State and local perspectives, who are the most frequent offenders with respect to electronic crime. Describing these offenders also posed a challenge. Exhibit 7 summarizes the information about whom State and local participants, based on their experiences, indicated are most frequently responsible for electronic crime.

Overall, sex crime offenders—those involved in exploiting children and distributing child pornography through the Internet—were cited most frequently (103 of the individuals prioritized it among the top three). A distant second were employees or insiders and criminal offenders. They received 69 and 67 "votes," respectively, for the top three choices. Hackers, mentioned 50 times, ranked fourth.

Two anomalies emerged from the groups' responses to the question of electronic crime offenders. Individuals meeting in the Western Region selected criminal offenders twice as often as Rocky Mountain Region and Northeastern Region officials and six times more frequently than the representatives meeting in the Southeastern Region. The explanation for this is uncertain. Conversely, southern jurisdictions appear to experience more problems with drug dealers pursuing their crime through electronic means than in any other region, but they have far fewer problems with criminal offenders.

One of the researchers' goals for this section was to ascertain the characteristics of the typical electronic offender. From discussions with State and local law enforcement officials and prosecutors, it is evident that there is no common description that can be applied to these offenders. There are different types of electronic crime offenders: employees, sex criminals, drug dealers, and common criminals. The one characteristic they have in common is that they use new electronic means to facilitate traditional crimes, such as theft, child pornography, and fraud. Several respondents suggested that the Federal Government may eventually need to profile electronic criminals in much the same way as the FBI currently does for serial killers and rapists.

This assessment was not intended to be an indepth, incident-based study of offenders who use computers to commit crimes; however, it allowed the researchers to derive a view of the socioeconomic characteristics of these criminals. In broad terms, electronic crime offenders tend to be males, ranging in age from the mid-teens to upper 50s, high school to college educated, middle to upper middle class, technically oriented, and skilled with a computer. This description does not vary significantly from region to region. Variances to the general description are apparent, however, when respondents describe hackers and criminal offenders. For example, hackers tend to be younger males and usually more skilled with a computer than the other types of offenders. Criminal offenders can be either male or female.

The following subsections summarize the characteristics of the top five types of electronic crime offenders, followed by a paragraph describing the remaining types, as defined by the participants.

Sex crime offenders. Of all the descriptions, the one for sex crime offenders drew the greatest consensus among the project participants. All the respondents described sex crime offenders as males. The age span is large: from 16 to 57, with the majority usually in their mid- to upper 30s and 40s. Sex

Exhibit 6. Most Frequent Electronic Crime Targets

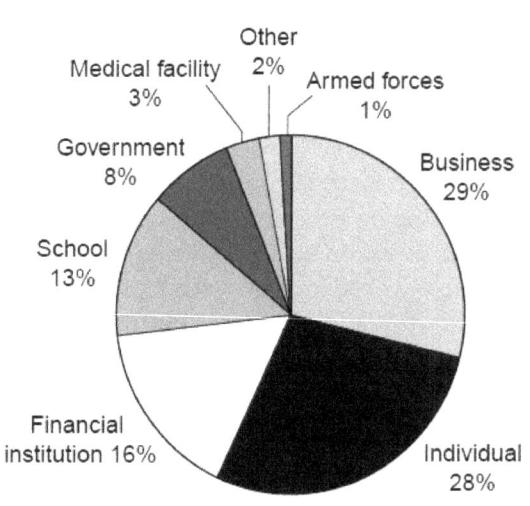

Note: Participant mentions totaled 360. Participants were asked to list their top three choices.

Exhibit 7. Most Frequent Electronic Crime Offenders

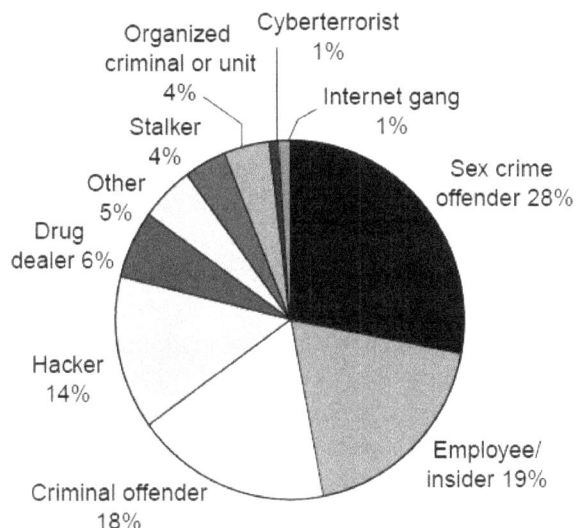

Note: Participant mentions totaled 360. Participants were asked to list their top three choices.

offenders operating through the Internet generally have at least a high school education; the majority received their college degrees. They tend to have moderate to high technical ability; have few, if any, prior arrests; and generally come from a middle-class background. Some are single while others are married; some have children. Many offenders frequently interact with young people or volunteer with local organizations and church groups.

Sex crime offenders also typically are described as loners or social outcasts who combine good organizational skills and recordkeeping abilities with meticulous and methodical attention to their criminality—specifically their efforts to lure children for sex—to lessen their chances of being targeted by the authorities. They also possess high-end computer equipment with large amounts of memory space to store thousands of pictures of high-quality resolution. They often employ sophisticated encryption technology, enabling them to secretly communicate with others involved with the child pornography underworld. In addition, more than any other offense, the computer and its associated technologies have enabled this crime to spread. The safe haven of the Internet and the privacy safeguards of society embolden these criminals. The anonymity that is

afforded sex criminals has opened doors to many people who otherwise would have hesitated to perpetrate such activity.

Employees or insiders. As with the sex crime offender description, there are no discernible regional differences with the employee or insider description. Of all the types, however, this is the most complex—employees or insiders who commit electronic crimes are of both genders, range in age from 20 to 45, come from all social and economic backgrounds, and are of all marital statuses (single, married, or divorced).

According to the participants, the typical employee or insider is in his or her mid-30s and harbors significant resentment toward his or her employer for a variety of reasons. The main motives are revenge and greed. These offenders are usually trusted employees who have easy access to the company's computer systems. Some have prior convictions, but for the most part they are first-time offenders. They have good computer skills, knowledge of the security features within the company, and an ability to mask their intrusions. Some of these offenders manipulate company information or attempt to destroy the information outright to harm the company's ability to conduct business.

The employees usually are longer term workers, work extra hours, and feel the company does not appreciate them or owes them something. Others, unlike their disgruntled counterparts, simply want more money than they are being paid, so they manipulate the company's payroll system out of greed. Some employees also engage in cargo theft of software, computers, or other electronic equipment from the company for monetary gain. State and local law enforcement officials cited numerous cases documenting the abovementioned examples.

Criminal offenders. The standard criminal offender, like that of the employee or insider, is of both genders. The age range generally is from the early 20s to the mid-40s, and their economic status and income tend to be low to middle class. Most criminal offenders are described as possessing average to advanced equipment and computer skills. The common underlying theme among all of them is their motive—greed. More often than not, criminal offenders have high rates of recidivism with prior convictions in forgery rings, credit card fraud, and stolen check-cashing schemes. These criminals use computers and other electronic means to enhance their ability to conduct these fraudulent activities and facilitate their operations.

Hackers. Of the five offenders described by the respondents, hackers comprise the youngest group. They tend to fall between the ages of 15 and 25 and almost always are males. They usually are intelligent and are social outcasts or loners—not unlike sex crime offenders. There was a consensus among the participants that hackers are the most technically superior of the offenders and usually are the most challenging for law enforcement to track. Their superior skills in masking their activities, not to mention the highly sophisticated equipment they use, present obstacles for all but the most well-equipped and -trained computer forensic units.

Many hackers have had previous problems in school or lack positive outlets for their talents. Many are college students who engage in such activity to relieve boredom or impress their friends, not necessarily to damage the computer or institution that they attack. Others are highly skilled criminals who use their expertise to unlawfully gain access to an institution's computer systems to maliciously wreak havoc or otherwise disrupt the flow of information. Their actions ultimately cause financial loss due to the cost of repairing damaged systems and the amount of time required to fix computers and other equipment that is rendered inoperable.

Drug dealers. Drug dealers are normally males in their early 20s to mid-30s who supplement their low- to mid-range incomes through criminal activity. The advent of new technology affords drug dealers more effective means with which to store their information as well as to conceal their communications by encrypting electronic messages and telephone conversations. They are not necessarily technically skilled; rather, they hire people to keep track of their transactions and handle the sophisticated communications equipment. They make use of high-end laptops, cellular phones, and other equipment that is easy to conceal and transport from one drug deal to the next.

Stalkers, organized criminals or units, cyberterrorists, and Internet gangs. The final category combines five types of electronic crime offenders that are not frequently encountered by State and local law enforcement. The information obtained from the field is inadequate to describe each offender in detail. Generally speaking, some organized crime elements employ sophisticated and advanced techniques as part of their modus operandi, such as encryption and hacking. They use these methods to conceal their activities, evade law enforcement, gather intelligence on others, or commit other crimes that support their illegal activities. Cyberstalkers also use advanced computers and equipment, enhancing their ability to mask their threatening, harassing, or criminal communications over the Internet. Internet gangs, including some hate groups, vary so significantly that a description of them would be almost impossible. Finally, cyberterrorists are rarely encountered by State and local law enforcement.

Support for electronic crime investigations

One of the most frequently heard complaints at the workshops pertained to awareness and support from upper level managers and policymakers. Although not the case universally, individuals holding upper management positions generally are older and usually have worked with computers at a basic level. Many of the respondents believed this in part explains why many senior officials do not fully appreciate the seriousness of the rapidly growing problem of electronic crime or what law enforcement needs to keep pace with these criminals. Of 122 responses, 84 indicated that managers are either unaware or only somewhat aware of computer crime issues.

"Managers are at the embryonic stage of understanding the importance of [electronic crime] because so many other crimes take precedence. This is viewed as victimless. You cannot take a picture of it or get your arms around it."

"The city councils are not aware—they could care less about [this type] of crime."

"In my case they [management] are very aware, but they can't necessarily do much about it

because it's a resource issue. There isn't enough funding and manpower to address the problem."

"Management awareness of electronic crime? . . . Can you say 'ostrich'?"

The first quote points to a real problem that electronic crime investigators confront. Working at the grassroots level, they have a good idea of the extent to which electronic intrusions and the criminal use of computers is occurring and how difficult it is to conduct forensic examinations and track the perpetrators. How does one sufficiently communicate that to others without concrete numbers to validate the problem? Statistics on drug crimes and homicides, for example, are not hard to find, and those data are routinely used to enhance law enforcement's capacity to counter those crimes. But there is currently no standard in place to systematically collect information about crimes committed against electronic systems or facilitated by these systems.

Significant underreporting of computer crimes

Most participants in the study believe that the vast majority of computer-related crimes are not reported to authorities as a criminal matter. For example, companies may choose to write off a loss, handle it internally, or pursue the case as a civil matter, according to the view of many participants. Since budgetmakers and policymakers rely heavily on numbers and on the priorities voiced by voters, the dearth of hard data and general awareness hurts most efforts to build stronger State and local crime control measures against electronic crime. Anecdotal information often is the only available evidence that can be used to capture management's attention. Many of those who participated in the assessment noted that if the actual losses and impact of computer-related crime could be studied and documented, the public and, by extension, public officials would begin to understand how serious this component of crime has become.

Profile of Types of Electronic Crimes and Investigation Needs

It is important to have case procedures in place to detect, investigate, and prosecute electronic crimes. In this section of the assessment, the researchers

asked State and local law enforcement officials and prosecutors to describe how they investigate crimes in which computers are involved. The researchers also wanted to know what tools and resources are being used and which ones are needed but currently unavailable either because of a lack of funds or because the agency has placed a low priority on purchasing the required tools.

Although all law enforcement agencies follow normal search-and-seizure protocols for evidence handling and investigations, many (though not a majority) rely on standard evidence collection procedures rather than on procedures uniquely tailored to electronic evidence. Because uniform electronic crime guidelines do not exist (as with NIJ's *Death Investigation: A Guide for the Scene Investigator*[3]), many agencies have adopted Federal guidelines.

Tools to detect and identify intrusion crimes

A large majority (75 percent) of the agencies involved in the assessment do not possess the necessary equipment or tools to effectively detect and identify computer or electronic intrusion crimes. There was a regional variance in this response. Of the 34 participants who answered this question in the Western Region, 15 claimed they are adequately equipped to detect and identify computer or electronic intrusion crimes. At each of the other three sites, few representatives believed they had sufficient resources. When queried about what tools they needed most, the answers covered everything from training to both basic and advanced tools (see "Commonly Identified Needs").

Profile of electronic crime

A major part of the effort in this section centered around which electronic crimes the agencies find most prevalent in their jurisdictions as well as which ones are the most challenging for their agencies to handle. To facilitate discussion, the types of crimes were grouped according to five categories:

- **Harmful content crimes**—crimes that include child pornography and child exploitation, stalking, harassment, threatening communications, proliferation of bomb-making information, and so forth.

- **Fraudulent activity**—crimes that cover telemarketing fraud, Internet fraud (e.g., online shopping schemes), electronic funds transfer fraud, electronic commerce fraud, and theft of identity.

- **Technology- or instrumentality-based crimes**—crimes, not including fraud, that employ advanced technology such as encryption to cloak criminal activities, organized crime, drug trafficking, economic or industrial espionage, and the like.

- **Hacking**—crimes that include malicious disruption of electronic systems or recreational thrill seekers.

- **National security threats**[4]—crimes that are primarily electronic attacks against critical infrastructures or are classified as cyberterrorism.

Harmful content crimes, particularly child pornography cases, ranked as the most prevalent. Agency representatives from all the regions spoke at length about the high incidence of this type of electronic crime. A close second was fraudulent activity, which is aided by the speed and connectivity of electronic systems. Those crimes classified as technology- or instrumentality-based ranked third, followed by hacking and national security threats. The last category understandably is not commonly encountered, nor is it the type of electronic-related crime that many non-Federal agencies would be expected to handle. It was included in this assessment in the event that a community may have been exposed to some form of cyberterrorism, particularly in terms of infrastructure attack.

Commonly Identified Needs

- Encryption-breaking technology
- Recovery equipment
- Forensic laboratory
- Courses on hacking
- Contacts for assistance
- Software to collect input and output data
- Office space
- Network intrusion detectors

There is a direct, inverse relationship between the rank order of the most prevalent and the most challenging electronic crimes. Most agency representatives believed that a threat to national security perpetrated electronically would be the most difficult to handle. Speaking from a base of experience on the remaining four categories, participants ranked hacking as a substantial challenge and noted that most hackers are extremely computer literate and competent. Close behind hacking was technology- or instrumentality-based crime, which frequently involves encryption technology and savvy criminals operating at the higher end of computer systems. Fraud committed through computers is not easy to solve, but it is less difficult than the higher ranked categories. Finally, while having the highest incidence among the categories of electronic crime, harmful content crimes were judged to be the least challenging to solve. Investigation experience is greater with this type of crime, and such experience is being shared among computer crime investigators. "Comparison of Electronic Crimes" presents the most prevalent and most challenging crimes.

Resources

Whether law enforcement agencies are pursuing a computer hacker or a child molester operating through the Internet, by and large they are poorly equipped and do not have adequate resources. Of the assessment participants, 112 told facilitators they need more training, 121 need an adequate number of personnel, and 130 need equipment—their top three priorities. Another finding is that 97 respondents evaluated their in-house ability to effectively deal with encrypted data as either "low" or "doesn't exist." This included basic and high-end decryption capabilities. The latter is rarely available at State and local levels. Basic decryption capabilities are primarily stymied because many jurisdictions do not have the funds to purchase the necessary software.

Forty-four of the representatives "frequently" or "always" use their own equipment to supplement that supplied by their agency. Budget constraints and lack of management awareness are the primary hindrances to acquiring more resources, according to participants.

"We have been waiting for money for a new photocopy machine for 3 months."

"It's hard to sell the boss on resources needed because it's hard to justify without data."

"Support from the community is lacking."

"There is no champion for this area of crime."

"There is way too much red tape within the agency."

"The political climate is not supportive."

"Management does not want to commit people full time to computer crimes."

"Our funding comes from forfeitures in other crimes—there needs to be direct funding for electronic crime units."

Exhibits 8 and 9, respectively, highlight the agencies' ability to handle encryption and the extent to which participants use their personal equipment to investigate electronic crime.

System Vulnerability, Critical Infrastructure, and Cyberterrorism

In May 1998, President Clinton signed Presidential Decision Directive 63 (PDD 63),[5] which called for a strategic plan to defend the Nation against cyberattacks. PDD 63 builds on the recommendations of the President's Commission on Critical Infrastructure Protection (PCCIP), chaired by Robert T. Marsh, which issued its report in October 1997.[6] PDD 63 is the culmination of an intense interagency effort to evaluate the recommendations from the Commission and produce a workable and innovative framework for critical infrastructure protection. The directive

Exhibit 8. Capability of Investigators to Handle Encrypted Evidence

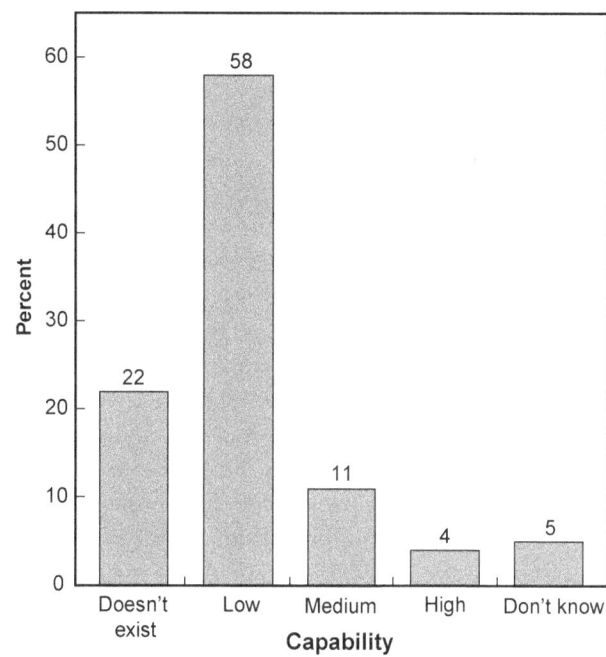

Note: 124 of 126 par icipants responded.

calls for an investment of $1.46 billion in fiscal year 2000 to defend the Nation's critical infrastructures. Critical infrastructures include power generation systems, banking and financial institutions, transportation networks, emergency services, and telecommunications. The directive also sets a goal of a reliable, interconnected, and secure information system infrastructure by 2003.

This section of the assessment was concerned with three areas. First, the researchers wanted to determine if any of the agencies represented had been victims of an electronic attack and, if so, what actions had been taken to prevent future attacks. Second, the researchers wanted to ascertain whether

Comparison of Electronic Crimes

Most Prevalent Crimes
- Harmful content crimes
- Fraudulent activity
- Technology- or instrumentality-based crimes
- Hacking
- National security threats

Most Challenging Crimes
- National security threats
- Hacking
- Technology- or instrumentality-based crimes
- Fraudulent activity
- Harmful content crimes

20

electronic attacks had occurred at any of the critical infrastructures and if the agency participants were aware of any response plans established with the critical infrastructure providers in their jurisdictions. Finally, the researchers were interested in determining how the participants perceived the level of interagency cooperation and intelligence sharing concerning potential cyberterrorist incidents.

This section was difficult to address in the field. As suggested earlier, most State and local law enforcement agencies do not have extensive experience in dealing with cyberterrorism or issues pertaining to critical infrastructure protection. Because a clear, delineated Federal response plan for cyberterrorism does not exist, there is a fundamental lack of understanding at the State and local levels in addressing this relatively recent threat. The uncertainty expressed by many of the participants when responding to questions posed during this section highlights the lack of awareness regarding critical infrastructure protection issues and cyberterrorism at the State and local levels. Many of the participants also had trouble

answering specific questions about access control and redundant systems because again the responsibility for systems security falls to the information technology (IT) department. Even within the same jurisdiction, agencies with related missions are not always communicating as well as they might. As one agency representative from the Rocky Mountain Region site noted, "No information is transferred or exchanged between us and the IT department."

System vulnerability

The widespread use of computers and the Internet has created the possibility for an individual to cause drastic harm to public health and safety by damaging or shutting down computers. Thirty-four participants stated that their computer systems had been accessed without authorization. Half of them were from the agencies that met in the Western Region. By comparison, only five participants from the Northeastern Region, six from the Southeastern Region, and seven from the Rocky Mountain

Exhibit 9. Extent to Which Personal Equipment Must Be Used

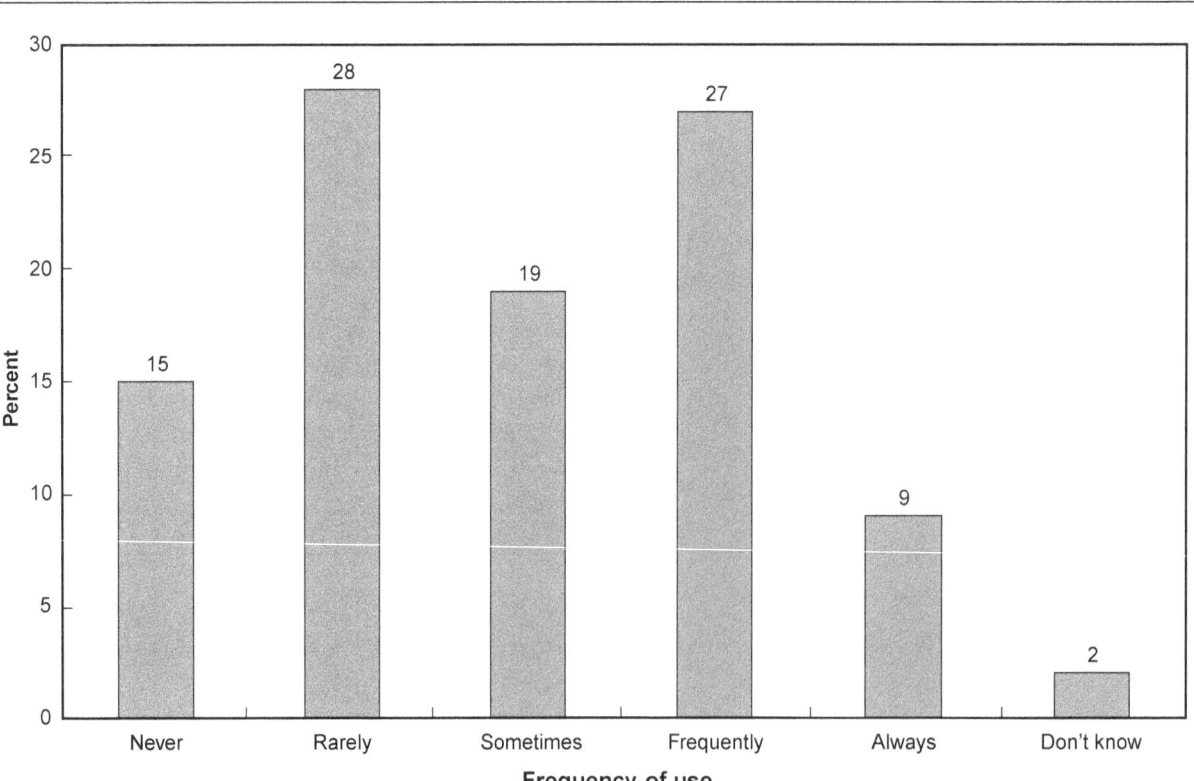

Note: 124 of 126 participants responded.

Region had experienced computer intrusions. In comparison, 51 participants said they had not experienced a computer intrusion, and 38 participants indicated they were not sure whether their systems had been accessed.

Regarding the means used to protect against a networked electronic intrusion, participants said their agencies employ audit trails, sniffers, investigative software, periodic inspections and monitoring, intrusion software, and other tools. Seventy-two percent of the representatives indicated their security systems have features that audit access to or disseminate sensitive information.

Systems can suffer from both external and internal intrusions. Three-quarters of the participants agreed that the threat of internal tampering is a concern and their agencies have taken actions to prevent this. "We are much more concerned with internal rather than external tampering of our agency's systems," one participant said. Indeed, at a June 1999 American Society for Industrial Security conference in Washington, D.C., Dr. Jerrold Post, a political psychology professor at George Washington University and a terrorism expert, noted that in industry, insiders continue to be the biggest threat. According to Dr. Post, the "use of information technology by insiders will increasingly become mainstreamed, both operationally and tactically."[7] According to the 1999 CSI/FBI survey, unauthorized access by insiders increased for the third straight year. In most cases, insiders are trusted employees and use that trust to gain access to systems without being monitored. The CSI/FBI survey revealed that 55 percent of respondents (out of 521) reported intrusions by insiders, while only 30 percent reported intrusions by perpetrators from the outside. In addition, 97 percent reported insider abuse of Internet access privileges.[8] These percentages seem to substantiate the finding that many agencies are vulnerable to insider abuse.

A number of individuals deferred to the IT staff for answers about how they deter internal intrusions. A few believed that no actions have been taken to prevent tampering from within, although it is a concern of their agencies. Background checks, passwords, built-in audit trails, new employee orientations, firewalls and protocols, keyword detection, and e-mail monitoring are some of the ways public safety agencies are protecting their electronic

systems from harm. One participant said he has "faith in the network people to keep the security strong at his agency." Exhibit 10 shows the percentage of agencies concerned with internal tampering of their systems.

According to the participants, it is not common practice for their law enforcement agencies to conduct formal periodic risk assessments of various security functions to deter electronic crimes. However, when risk assessments are carried out on a regular basis, they generally are conducted for physical security functions and communications security. Personnel and operations risk assessments happen less frequently. About half of the study participants say their agencies have a plan in place in the event their network communications systems are rendered inoperable, although 22 percent were not certain.

Critical infrastructure and cyberterrorism

In October 1997, the President's Commission on Critical Infrastructure Protection noted:

> A satchel of dynamite and a truckload of fertilizer and diesel fuel are known terrorist tools. Today, the right command sent over a

Exhibit 10. Is Internal Tampering a Concern?

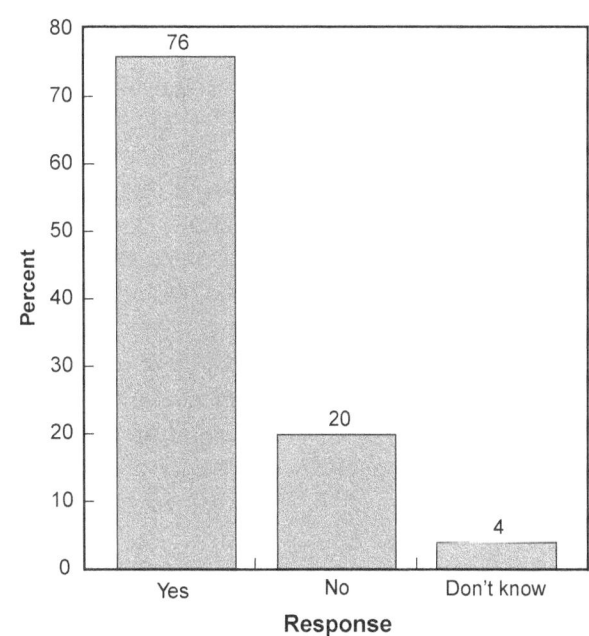

Note: 125 of 126 participants responded.

network to a power generation station's control computer could be just as devastating as a backpack full of explosives, and the perpetrator would be more difficult to identify and apprehend.[9]

The difficulties encountered by law enforcement in identifying and apprehending perpetrators of a cyberterrorist incident pale in comparison to larger obstacles such as multijurisdictional coordination and cooperation and law enforcement operations and mindsets that are sometimes steeped in antiquated procedures.

Law enforcement has become accustomed to dealing with threats in the physical world, but it will increasingly need to cope with emerging threats in the cyberworld. According to terrorism expert Dr. Neil Livingstone in an American Society for Industrial Security speech given in Arlington, Virginia, in June 1999, "The Carlos [the Jackal] of the future will be someone with a laptop." As one of the participants in the survey discussed in this Research Report noted, "This arena [cyberterrorism] is unexplored at the State and local levels." The tools and methods that have assisted law enforcement in combating traditional crime will no longer suffice in the years ahead. Outdated methods and operations will eventually need to give way to new ones geared toward crime in the Information Age. The Commission report summarized this need for new thinking when it stated:

> Because it may be impossible to determine the nature of a threat until after it has materialized, infrastructure owners and operators— most of whom are in the private sector— must focus on protecting themselves against the tools of disruption, while the government helps by collecting and disseminating the latest information about those tools and their employment. This cooperation implies a more intimate level of mutual communication, accommodation, and support than has characterized public-private sector relations in the past.[10]

Indeed, the private sector and government will need to cooperate to defend our critical infrastructures from attacks.

A national protection plan cannot be accomplished without private and public partnerships because many of the key targets for cyberattacks—power and telecommunications grids, financial flows, and transportation systems—are in private hands. Public involvement is not only a role for the Federal Government. State and local governments must be involved because they own and operate many of the critical infrastructures and their agencies often are the first responders to a crisis.

Forty-five of the participants were aware of instances in which the computer or electronic system of a local infrastructure was attacked. Targets have included the telecommunications system, banks, emergency services, and government services. Intelligence sharing among law enforcement agencies is important to solving all types of crime. Study participants generally agreed that cooperation among law enforcement agencies in terms of potential cyberterrorist incidents or those involving unauthorized access and malicious disruption of network computer systems is adequate. However, some clearly believe the intelligence-sharing apparatus currently in place requires considerable improvement.

"The Feds should be saying, 'Let us help you.' There needs to be a partnership between State and local law enforcement agencies and the Feds regarding cyberterrorism."[11]

"The more information and intelligence that is given to us ahead of time, the more prepared we are to make an effective decision and take appropriate action."

"National security threats are not necessarily challenging to handle in terms of technical challenges, but more so because of the jurisdictional problems that occur."

To ensure that all areas potentially related to cyberterrorism were covered in the assessment, the participants were asked an open question: What other areas related to cyberterrorism need to be addressed? They offered excellent suggestions and insights on many approaches, but the most frequently mentioned need was for stronger cooperation with industry to combat cyberterrorism.

"Some of the Internet service providers are not always keeping the necessary records so that law enforcement can track cyberterrorists."

"A lot of people don't realize the significance of this [cyberterrorism], especially when dealing with extremist groups."

Forensic Evidence Collection and Analysis

Properly seizing and processing electronic evidence is critical to making a good case that prosecutors can accept for prosecution. The researchers were interested in how State and local law enforcement agencies are handling electronic evidence, from the crime scene to the laboratory. A majority of the agencies represented follow special procedures for collecting electronic evidence. As one participant noted, "It's a crime scene within a crime scene" and, therefore, must be handled as such. For example, electronic evidence needs to be separately maintained in a controlled environment and requires unique tools and expertise to analyze. The Computer Crime and Intellectual Property Section at the U.S. Department of Justice identifies four challenges.

Finding evidence in the information ocean. Advances in technology will soon provide all Americans with access to a powerful, high-capacity network that will transport all their communications (including voice and video), deliver entertainment, allow access to information, and permit storage of large quantities of information most anywhere. In such an environment, finding important evidence can be nearly impossible. Separating valuable information from irrelevant information, for either communications or stored data, requires extraordinary technical efforts. Determining the location where evidence is stored is also quite difficult; electronic surveillance is often necessary but is made difficult by anonymity, the lack of traceability, and encryption.

Anonymity. Computer networks permit persons to easily maintain anonymity, which prevents accountability and thus tempts people to commit crimes who would otherwise not break the law out of fear of being caught. The problem with the Internet is that everyone knows everyone else's "name" but not who they really are. Much like the citizen band

radio craze of the 1980s, most Web surfers have a "handle," a false name or identity. As a result, the types of crimes that are facilitated by anonymity, such as making threats and manipulating stocks, are expected to increase as more people realize computers allow them anonymity.

Traceability. Related to anonymity, traceability refers to how difficult it is to establish the source and destination of communications on computers and communications networks, such as the Internet. Because everything on the Internet is based on communications, traceability is essential to determining identity in cases arising from it. However, traceability is becoming more difficult because of the proliferation and easy availability of multiple communications providers. Communications on the Internet, for example, can easily pass through 10 different providers (such as America Online and AT&T), each of which must provide information (often in real time) to trace a communication.

Encryption. Shortly, the vast majority of data and communications will be encrypted. This will assist in protecting data confidentiality of law-abiding persons, but as criminals also increasingly adopt this technology, law enforcement will be less able to obtain communications and stored data for investigations.

An official at the Western Region meetings remarked that a member of his electronic crime unit has to be present to collect the evidence. Another representative mentioned that "evidence is treated like evidence, but electronic evidence is different because they only keep backups, not originals." Rocky Mountain Region participants commented that digital evidence differs from other physical evidence because it is easily altered or changed and therefore must be handled more carefully, preferably by a specially trained person. In general, it was acknowledged that every type of evidence has its own set of protocols that varies according to the type of evidence involved. Many agencies only now are in the process of drafting special procedures for electronic evidence handling.

A large majority (73 percent) of the individuals involved in the field meetings have received training on the collection of electronic evidence. When asked whether evidence analysis and reports could be fast tracked on priority cases where an arrest or indictment is imminent, 65 percent said this could be done, 25 percent said no, and 10 percent did not know. Thus, even if the laboratory turnaround time is generally slow, when needed, the evidence results can be provided quickly more often than not.

Field personnel use various types of laboratories to process and examine seized computers and digital evidence recovered at a crime scene, ranging from laboratories internal to the agencies to Federal and private industry laboratories.

A majority (57 percent) of participants believed that laboratories follow a standard operating procedure or protocol particular to the examination of electronic evidence; however, 23 percent said they did not believe this was true, and 20 percent were not sure. More participants (60 percent) than not commented that the laboratories they use do not have sufficient capability to process and analyze the cases submitted to them. Many complained that the laboratories are understaffed, lack advanced equipment for "higher end" analysis, have insufficient space, need better trained examiners for advanced analysis, and require more tools for decryption. "We are literally running a shoestring operation,"

Exhibit 11. Capability of Laboratories to Decipher Encrypted Evidence

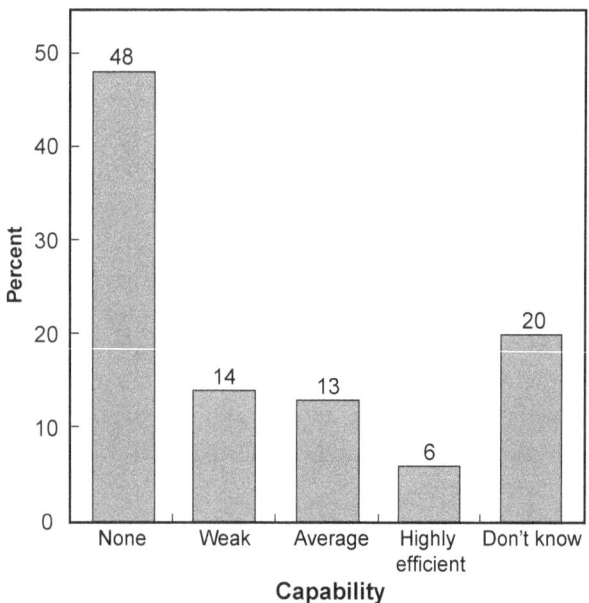

Note: 122 of 126 par icipants responded.

---

admitted one of the Rocky Mountain Region site participants. In the Southeastern Region, one of the officials present commented on his agency's own limitations, "We don't have the training to even know what to ask for."

Encrypted evidence poses a special challenge. Sixty-two percent of the respondents told the facilitators that their ability to work with encrypted evidence is weak or nonexistent, and 20 percent were unsure of their laboratory's capabilities. Exhibit 11 shows how State and local participants evaluated laboratory capabilities vis-a-vis encrypted data.

This inability to handle encrypted evidence is especially noteworthy in light of recent studies on the use of encryption for criminal purposes. The 1997 report by Dorothy E. Denning and William E. Baugh, Jr., *Encryption and Evolving Technologies as Tools of Organized Crime and Terrorism,* states that the total number of criminal cases involving encryption worldwide is increasing at an annual growth rate of 50 to 100 percent.[12] Encryption is an effective tool to protect privacy when used lawfully. However, it can hinder law enforcement investigations and increase costs because of the problems associated with cracking the encryption.

According to the Denning and Baugh study, encryption also poses challenges in terms of terrorist threats. The study's central claim is the following:

> [T]he impact of encryption on crime and terrorism is at its early stages. . . . Encryption policy must effectively satisfy a range of interests: information security, public safety, law and order, national security, the economic competitiveness of industry in a global market, technology leadership, and civil liberties.[13]

Law enforcement will need to increase its encrypted evidence capability if it expects to keep pace with criminals. The participants discussed what would enhance their capabilities in working with electronic evidence. Some of the most widely shared requests included:

- Nationally recognized standards for handling, collecting, and analyzing electronic evidence.

- Portable laboratories.

- Technical support for investigations, including a central repository of information for reference and networking.

- Guidelines on what a laboratory should acquire.

- Nontraditional operating systems training.

- Technical assistance.

- Improved analytical software to speed up the examination process.

- Joint training for investigators and attorneys.

- Legislative awareness to garner support for funding laboratories to increase electronic evidence analysis capabilities.

- Training in evidence search and seizure.

- Wireless communication capability.

- Patrol officer training.

- Clearinghouse of electronic crime cases.

- Library of hardware and software.

- Dedicated resources for computer crimes.

Legal Issues and Prosecution

During the past decade, the use of computers and the Internet has grown exponentially, and individuals have increasingly become dependent on technology in their daily lives. Yet as computer use has blossomed, so too have criminals increasingly exploited computers to commit crimes and to threaten the safety and security of others. Deterring and punishing such wrongdoing requires a legal structure that will support detection and successful prosecution of offenders. The laws defining computer offenses and the legal tools needed to properly investigate such crimes have lagged behind technological and social changes.

State and local law enforcement entities will face ever-increasing challenges in investigating and prosecuting Internet and other high-tech crimes. This is because the Internet and high-tech telecommunications have created an environment in which interpersonal and commercial relationships increasingly will involve interstate and international transactions, but State and local authorities remain bound by much narrower jurisdictional limitations on their investigative authority.

For example, Missouri could have 20 victims who complain to their State attorney general about a "failure to render" Internet scam that took their money, $250 each for a complete personal computer system, a total loss of $5,000. The Web site they ordered from and sent money to is located in Florida. But the FBI in St. Louis does not want to pursue fraud cases unless they meet the prosecution guidelines threshold of $25,000. The Missouri attorney general issues a subpoena to the service provider in Florida for basic account information (i.e., who pays for the Web site). How can this subpoena be enforced? The same question arises if bank records in another State are being sought.

Currently there is no formal legal mechanism to allow for the enforcement of State subpoenas in other States. Cooperation can be achieved when one State attorney general's office voluntarily assists a sister State authority in either serving an out-of-State subpoena or seeking an in-State court order to enforce the out-of-State subpoena. However, the reliability and consistency of this procedure is not uniform, and the ability to secure enforcement of an out-of-State subpoena on a recalcitrant party is questionable at best.

To enhance the authority of State and local law enforcement to investigate cybercrimes that are too small to justify the investment of Federal resources but nevertheless require interstate process, more effective tools are required for enforcing State subpoenas in other jurisdictions. There are at least two possible models for creating these tools. One model is to develop an interstate compact that would establish procedures for signatory States to follow in enforcing out-of-State subpoenas. The Uniform Act to Secure the Attendance of Witnesses from Without a State in Criminal Proceedings is a comparable legal regime that has been adopted in the 50 States, the District of Columbia, Puerto Rico, and the Virgin Islands (e.g., D.C. Code 1981, §§ 23–1501–1504).

A second model involves a Federal statute empowering the Federal courts to issue "full faith and credit" orders enforcing out-of-State criminal subpoenas. This alternative might avoid the complexities of developing and adopting an interstate agreement, but it could possibly raise federalism concerns. Whichever type of approach is pursued, action is necessary in this area to ensure that victims of Internet crime have an effective recourse to which they can turn for protection and enforcement.

In addition, one Federal statute has hindered computer crime investigations for most Federal, State, and local investigators. The Privacy Protection Act (PPA) has shielded criminal activities from legitimate law enforcement investigations. This unintended consequence of PPA has resulted from the exponential growth in computer use during the last decade. With the advent of the Internet and widespread computer use, almost any computer can be used, in effect, to "publish" materials. Thus, although Congress intended to limit government searches of places such as newspaper offices when it passed PPA in 1980, currently the act potentially applies to almost every search of any computer. Moreover, because computers now commonly contain enormous data storage devices, wrongdoers can use them to store material for publication—material that PPA protects—while simultaneously storing child pornography, stolen classified documents, or other contraband or evidence of crime.

Notwithstanding the best efforts of those involved in crafting the Electronic Communication Privacy Act (ECPA) in 1986, the statute no longer effectively balances the competing interests of telecommunications users, service providers, and the legitimate needs of government investigators. The problems principally stem from two factors: the explosive growth of the Internet and inconsistencies and gaps in ECPA itself. With the widespread use of computers and the Internet, the proportion of criminal activity occurring online or with telecommunications technologies has increased enormously. E-mail, voice mail, user access logs, and remotely stored files play an important—and in many cases, critical—role in investigating and prosecuting crimes ranging from extortion and murder to large-scale consumer fraud.

This section of the research was designed to determine agency awareness about the legal issues of electronic crime, prosecutor concerns about preparing and presenting this type of case, and resource requirements for courtroom presentations. Indications from the participants show that the great majority (73 percent) have someone on staff who is knowledgeable about the legal issues, procedures, and laws affecting electronic crime investiga-

tions and prosecutions. Although most jurisdictions are operating with a good understanding of the laws and rules of procedure on electronic crime, the majority (66 percent) find that the laws themselves have not kept pace with the increasing complexities of electronic crime. Exhibit 12 depicts these results.

"I think it is impossible for the laws to keep pace . . . the technology is changing too rapidly."

The overriding theme throughout the discussions was that current laws do not encompass the new ways that crimes are being committed. Moreover, a wide disparity exists among the States in what is considered to be an electronic crime. What is a felony in one jurisdiction is a misdemeanor in another, which complicates extradition requests and cooperation among law enforcement agencies. According to one participant, the lack of commitment to sustaining an electronic crime unit is driven somewhat by the fact that the laws dealing with electronic crime are not stringent enough. Some people within law enforcement, according to this participant, have to deal with the following mindset: "I could put you in tennis shoes, and you could go out and get felony drug arrests. Why should I pay for computers and training to get misdemeanors?"

Exhibit 12. Are Laws Keeping Pace With Electronic Crimes?

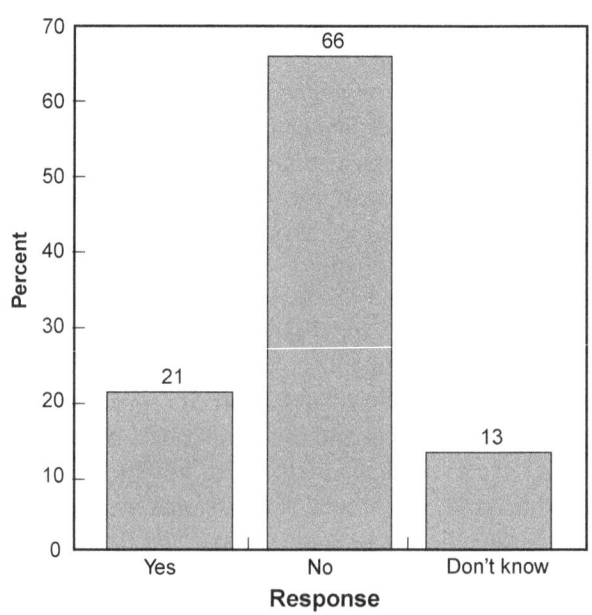

Note: 122 of 126 par icipants responded.

All the groups offered suggestions for how the laws and legal system could be improved so that criminals can be held more accountable for their actions. The list of ideas covered many issues, such as the need to change laws to allow for more wiretaps.

"Those drafting the laws should be close to those working the crimes. . . . [T]hey do not understand the technology they are writing laws about."

"We still have legislatures dealing with 8-track tape technology."

"Computer crimes need to be upgraded from misdemeanors to felonies."

"The issues surrounding electronic crime are specific and complex, and the laws are too broad to address the issues."

"The legislative process needs to be speeded up to keep laws in pace with technology changes."

"We need more laws dealing with the Internet."

"Penalties need to be harsher."

"The States should adopt some of the Federal laws dealing with electronic crime."

Investigators and prosecutors feel stymied, not only by inadequate laws but with the challenges involved in presenting technical electronic evidence in the courtroom. Here again, many participants expressed concern that awareness, training, and resources are lacking on the prosecution side as well as on the investigation side. Generally, the participants believe that if a case is too complex, it will not be prosecuted. "Prosecutors are not comfortable with the topic" and "Prosecutors have a hard time explaining technical terms to a jury" were commonly voiced opinions. Difficulties in presenting these cases occur not simply because a prosecutor may be unfamiliar with electronic terminology and systems but because jury members may be even less knowledgeable. A serious concern is the extent to which evidence can be simplified for the purposes of presentation without inadvertently crossing the line to tampering.

"Presenting technical evidence to a nontechnical audience is the biggest problem. It takes too much time and energy to present the evidence, and we do not have enough funding to support it."

Among the attorneys represented in the groups, several called for more sophisticated courtroom presentation equipment. "We have to be proactive in coming up with different models for presenting evidence in the court," stated one district attorney. Another mentioned that a media presentation unit within the agency was needed to handle technical presentations. A special course on electronic crime and case presentation concepts for prosecutors was a well-received suggestion by prosecutors and investigators alike. Vertical prosecution for electronic crime was proposed by one participant, an idea most applicable to larger jurisdictions with sizable caseloads.

Many ideas were circulated about how to further the successful investigation and prosecution of electronic crime cases. Participants consistently supported the view that the Internet should eventually be regulated by Federal laws, particularly sex sites, "otherwise child exploitation crimes will continue to rise." Echoing that opinion, another participant stated: "Nothing can prevent kids from accessing these [pornographic] sites. Federal law, therefore, must regulate the Internet, or these problems will continue to get worse."

In the Southeastern Region, participants called for technical assistance and information on case studies of successfully prosecuted cases and electronic presentations in court, list servs, software libraries, and general resource sharing among electronic crime investigators and prosecutors nationwide. The representatives meeting in the Western Region concurred with those ideas and also called for high-quality experts who can be called on for assistance and immediate access to specific case findings for Federal and State case law and discovery findings. Other solutions forwarded from the Western Region included standardizing the training offered in electronic crime, establishing dedicated computer crime units, and clearly defining what constitutes a forensic expert. Better defense training also was suggested as a way to avoid future appeals for incompetent or ineffective defense.

The meetings in the Northeastern Region drew suggestions for prosecutor training, computer forensics laboratories, and better equipment to use in court. In the Rocky Mountain Region, a significant emphasis was placed on increased cooperation and networking between organizations and States. Several participants want to see statewide teams with subject matter experts to answer questions and help solve case problems.

"A rapid procurement policy for electronic crime case resources [is needed]."

"Undercover capability to conduct proactive, online investigations [is necessary]."

Training

The availability of electronic crime training—at all levels—was a concern heard consistently from participants throughout the country. In particular, more training at both the basic and advanced levels is needed to ensure that electronic crime cases are adequately identified and brought to trial. A large majority (75 percent) of the officials who participated have received some electronic crime training.

Deficiencies appear to be for entry-level patrol officers (e.g., preventing inadvertent harm, protecting the electronic crime scene) and for upper level computer forensics specialists. Awareness training for prosecutors, politicians, and judges ranks high on the needs list as well. Only 37 percent of the agencies represented offer basic computer crime awareness and evidence collection training to entry-level or front-line personnel. Exhibit 13 shows whether training in electronic crime has been received, and if so, the topics that were covered.

"Basic electronic crime training for all officers is vital."

"Technical assistance is needed for the front-line officers and street cops to deal with electronic crimes that are occurring more frequently."

One issue that can seriously affect training is the potential for turnover within the unit as promotions occur. Often, a jurisdiction's promotion policies undermine the retention of uniquely trained and experienced personnel. The loss is felt most keenly

Exhibit 13. Training Received, by Topic

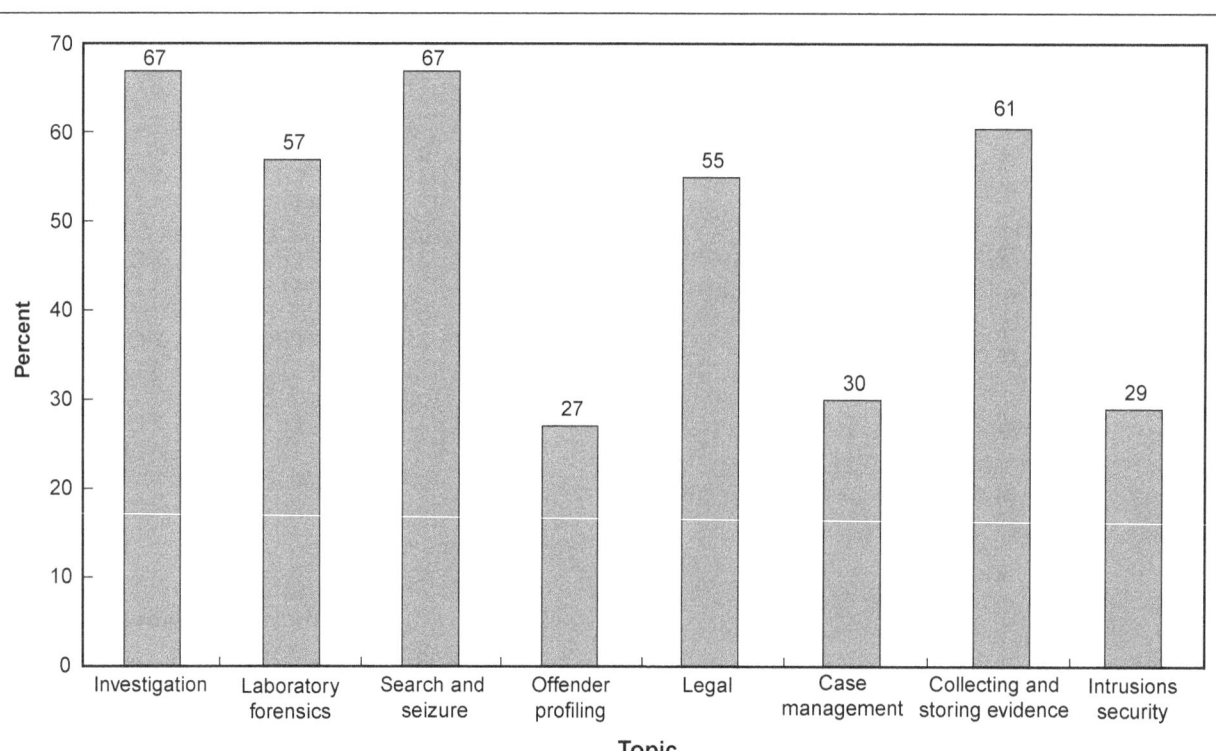

Note: 75 percent of participants reported receiving electronic crime training.

in special operations units in which there has been a heavy investment in training. New personnel must be "trained up," which is time consuming and expensive. Nearly 80 percent of the participants indicated that it would not or might not be possible to advance in their careers while remaining in the electronic crime field.

"Promotion means I go back to patrolling the streets."

"I lost two highly trained people to promotion. Now how do I replace that knowledge base?"

Retaining trained electronic investigators and laboratory personnel is a problem at all levels of government. Expertise is lost, not only to promotions and transfers but to the private sector, where the appeal of higher pay and, often, shorter hours attracts many specially qualified personnel.

Respondents identified more than two dozen sponsors of the training they have received, including the Agora Group, American Society for Industrial Security, Association of Certified Fraud Examiners, Computer Analysis Response Team, FBI, Federal Computer Investigation Committee, Federal Emergency Management Agency, Forensic Association of Computer Technologists, High Technology Crime Investigation Association, International Association of Chiefs of Police, International Association of Computer Investigative Specialists, National Association of Attorneys General, National White Collar Crime Center, NLECTC–Northeast, and State Departments of Justice.

Many agencies and associations are responding to the growing need for electronic crime and evidence training by offering a plethora of seminars and training. A national certification program would establish professional levels of skill and knowledge and would serve as the basis for future course development. State and local practitioners also want input into what the electronic crime training course priorities should be to ensure their needs are being fulfilled. (See "Training Topics Suggested by Participants.")

The respondents believed that field courses offered on site will have the highest value to them, followed closely by courses at in-residence regional training sites. Even though the quality of in-residence Federal courses (e.g., at the FBI or the Bureau of Alcohol, Tobacco and Firearms) is ranked high, these courses are not easily accessible for many jurisdictions not on the East Coast, and they place strict limitations on who can attend. Airfare costs alone can place these courses out of reach. Training provided through satellite hookups and on CD-ROM are valuable as a supplement to other forms of training, according to the participants, and probably the only viable option in more remote, less populated jurisdictions.

The topic about which there was the most significant consensus is that the gap in public- and private-sector information and resource sharing is wide. The participants noted that private industry can be a resource, insofar as identifying electronic crime incidents and having the technology to help investigate them. The vast majority of participants expressed concern that electronic crime units and industry function as completely separate entities, with only occasional overlap, such as in the sampling of existing private-public task forces generally found in southern California. It is widely held that bringing in the private sector is vital. Some participants specifically noted how important it is for the

Training Topics Suggested by Participants

- Forensic tools
- Undercover (cyber) investigations training
- Hacks, cracks, and profiling
- Front-line officer training
- Politician and supervisor training
- Intrusions and security training
- Operating systems and network training
- Evidence collection and processing
- Network expertise
- Password and encryption training
- Prosecutor training
- Systems analysis training
- Search-and-seizure training

private sector to keep law enforcement in mind when developing cybertools.

Several participants offered examples of industry's efforts to cooperate, including a special resource pool in Austin, Texas. Microsoft, for example, has a 24-hour, 7-day-per-week hotline to respond to all concerns about electronic crime relating to its products.

Notes

1. Power, Richard, Computer Security Issues & Trends: 1999 CSI/FBI *Computer Crime and Security Survey* 5 (1) (Winter 1999): 1.

2. Ibid., 3.

3. National Medicolegal Review Panel, *Death Investigation: A Guide for the Scene Investigator,* Research Report, Washington, DC: U.S. Department of Justice, National Institute of Justice, November 1999, NCJ 167568.

4. As mentioned previously, Federal law enforcement has the lead role in a cyberterrorist incident or an attack that affects the Nation's critical infrastructures. State and local law enforcement agencies have minimal experience with this type of electronic crime.

5. *The Clinton Administration's Policy on Critical Infrastructure Protection: Presidential Decision Directive 63,* White Paper, 1998. Retrieved October 4, 2000, from the World Wide Web: http://www.whitehouse.gov/WH/EOP/NSC/html/documents/NSCDoc3 html.

6. President's Commission on Critical Infrastructure Protection, *Critical Foundations: Protecting America's Infrastructures,* Washington, DC: President's Commission on Critical Infrastructure Protection, 1997.

7. Post, Jerrold, speech given at the American Society for Industrial Security Conference, Washington, D.C., June 1999.

8. Power, *Computer Security Issues & Trends,* 4.

9. President's Commission on Critical Infrastructure Protection, *Critical Foundations,* x.

10. Ibid., x.

11. This is the same recommendation as that from NIJ's earlier assessment of State and local needs to combat terrorism of all types. See National Institute of Justice, *Inventory of State and Local Law Enforcement Technology Needs to Combat Terrorism,* Research in Brief, Washington, DC: U.S. Department of Justice, National Institute of Justice, January 1999, NCJ 173384.

12. Denning, Dorothy E., and William E. Baugh, Jr., *Encryption and Evolving Technologies as Tools of Organized Crime and Terrorism,* Washington, DC: National Strategy Information Center, 1997.

13. Ibid.

Commentary and the Critical Ten

Electronic crimes and the ability of law enforcement in the United States to detect, investigate, and prosecute these incidents are areas of increasing concern. It is generally held that the United States is at risk from domestic and international threats. State and local law enforcement participants who contributed to this assessment provided a firsthand perspective of the technology, policies, research, training, and direct assistance they require to combat electronic crime. The participants related their experiences with electronic crime and their concerns for the future. In doing so, they provided valuable insight and information about all aspects of the problem.

The Critical Ten

The participants mentioned dozens of needs for all aspects of combating electronic crime, which were documented, categorized, and evaluated. Ten areas of concern dominated the discussions, and they are identified as the "Critical Ten" (See "The Critical Ten").

In addition to the top 10 needs, two overarching issues emerged from this assessment. Whether the need is high-end computer forensic training or onsite task force development assistance, progress needs to be accomplished quickly and in a coordinated manner through a centralized gateway. Why the sense of urgency and the focus on coordination? Simply put, the window of opportunity for law enforcement to at least keep pace with electronic crime (let alone get ahead of the problem) is quite short. Mostly, this is because the capacity of technology being used in the commission of electronic crimes is increasing exponentially and at a pace that significantly challenges the resources of criminal justice agencies. The emphasis on a coordinated approach is both practical and logical—there is little time to accomplish a lot with limited resources. Therefore, time is of the essence in crafting and implementing solutions.

The most important aspect of these unique challenges is time sensitivity. Unless a national effort is launched expeditiously, electronic crimes likely will outpace the resources of most State and local law enforcement agencies.

To maximize investments in new or expanded tools, training, onsite assistance, and research, the U.S. Department of Justice's mission to assist criminal justice agencies in supporting electronic crime and counterterrorism initiatives should be carried out in full.

The Critical Ten needs are described below; they are not prioritized.

Critical need 1: Public awareness

A solid information and awareness program is needed to educate the general public, elected and appointed officials, and the private sector about the incidence and impact of electronic crime.

The Critical Ten

1. Public awareness

2. Data and reporting

3. Uniform training and certification courses

4. Onsite management assistance for electronic crime units and task forces

5. Updated laws

6. Cooperation with the high-tech industry

7. Special research and publications

8. Management awareness and support

9. Investigative and forensic tools

10. Structuring a computer crime unit

With many cases undetected or unreported and with the dearth of hard data on electronic crime trends, most individuals are unaware of the extent to which their lives, financial status, businesses, families, or privacy might be affected by electronic crime. Neither are most people aware of how quickly the threat is growing. A multifaceted information and awareness campaign is needed to clearly document and publicize how electronic crimes affect our society. Unless the public is made aware of the growing use of technology to commit crimes, cybercriminals will continue to steal people's money, personal identities, and property.

Critical need 2: Data and reporting

More comprehensive data are needed to establish a clearer picture of the extent and impact of electronic crime and to monitor trends.

In response to the Computer Fraud and Abuse Act, the FBI amended its Uniform Crime Reporting (UCR) Program to address electronic crime. It placed a question in the National Incident-Based Reporting System (NIBRS) to document if a criminal offender used a computer in the commission of a crime. However, additional details about the use of computers in crime are needed to measure fully the incidence of electronic crime.

Without more data, detailed analysis, or a crime victimization study, it is difficult to track regional or national trends in electronic crime. Hard data are needed to better understand this era of electronic crime and to communicate it to budgetmakers and policymakers as well as to citizens.

Of interest is the extent to which "traditional" crimes (such as fraud, theft, forgery, and drug trafficking) involve the use of a computer. It also is critical to document "new" crime vis-a-vis electronic systems; for example, a cyberattack. Debate is under way about whether society should consider expanding the current crime classifications— "crimes against persons" and "crimes against property"—to include a third, "crimes against such intangibles as information, data, and communications." Currently, there is no method to classify these offenses at the crime index level.

Critical need 3: Uniform training and certification courses

Law enforcement officers and forensic scientists need specific levels of training and certification to correctly carry out their respective roles when investigating electronic crimes, collecting and examining evidence, and providing courtroom testimony. This training should reflect State and local priorities. Prosecutors, judges, probation and parole officers, and defense attorneys also need basic training in electronic crime.

Both entry-level and advanced training are needed for law enforcement officers and investigators, prosecutors and defense attorneys, probation and parole officers, and judges. First-line officers who secure the initial crime scene need training on basic forensic evidence recognition and collection techniques. National standards should be developed and applied toward a certification program that ensures uniform skill levels. Prosecutors and judges require awareness training and case histories on electronic crime incidents.

State and local law enforcement representatives noted repeatedly that advanced computer and forensics-related classes are difficult to find. Another concern was that the level of sophistication of the equipment, software tools, and training needed far exceeds the budgets of most departments. This is especially problematic for courses offered out of State. Attendance is expensive in terms of both personnel time and tuition, travel, and per diem costs.

Within the U.S. Department of Justice, three resources support State and local law enforcement information training requirements. The National Cybercrime Training Partnership (NCTP)—an organization chaired by the Computer Crime and Intellectual Property Section of the Department of Justice and involving partners from Federal, State, and local law enforcement agencies—has responded by placing the development and delivery of priority courses dealing with electronic crime on the fast track. The National White Collar Crime Center (NW3C) located in Fairmont, West Virginia, serves as the operations center for NCTP. NW3C provides a full-time staff and consists of highly skilled instructors, curriculum development specialists, and researchers to support the training needs of State and local law enforcement agencies around the country. NIJ's National Law Enforcement and Corrections Technology Center system provides clearinghouses for State and local electronic crime training. The centers are located throughout the country and are an important focal and outreach mechanism for the delivery of electronic crime training.

Another avenue of approach that State and local agencies can consider adopting is the Cyber Corps concept. Cyber Corps addresses the shortage of highly skilled computer science programmers in the Federal Government by enabling agencies to recruit a cadre of experts to respond to attacks on computer networks. As planned, individuals pursuing a computer security education would receive financial aid in return for a commitment to work after graduation for the U.S. Government.

Critical need 4: Onsite management assistance for electronic crime units and task forces

State and local law enforcement agencies need immediate assistance in developing computer investigation units, creating regional computer forensics capabilities, organizing task forces, and establishing programs with private industry.

A majority of the agencies represented in this study called for a county (or regional) investigative task force approach to the technically challenging and time-consuming job of investigating crimes involving computers. Agencies are seeking hands-on assistance from experts in electronic crime and in criminal task force development to enhance their ability to combat electronic crimes at all levels. Simply stated, investigative task forces are an extremely effective tool in fighting crime, as has been proven with drug and arson task forces.

Direct assistance in forming electronic crime task forces is urgently needed for several reasons. Specially trained examiners and dedicated, costly equipment are needed to analyze the evidence contained in a computer's hard drive and recover the data elements pertinent to a criminal case. Electronic evidence is likely to implicate individuals from other, often distant, jurisdictions. Also, for

many prosecutors, presenting high-tech evidence in court is challenging in terms of both ferreting through highly technical terms and making it understandable for the jury.

Combining forces among agencies makes it more affordable to acquire the high-tech tools used in analyzing computer evidence and to coordinate strategies and procedures to deal with electronic crime. State and local agencies suggest that through task forces, investigators from neighboring jurisdictions can pool their knowledge, sponsor training, and collaborate on cases. They can adopt a standard investigation protocol and reporting format that in turn would make it easier for prosecutors to evaluate the merits of cases. Suggestions on how to begin a dialogue with business and industry and to engender partnerships with them should be included in any technical assistance provided to criminal justice agencies. The experience of interagency task forces that operate to solve other complex crimes, such as arson, offer strategies that could be applied to electronic crime task forces.

Critical need 5: Updated laws

Effective, uniform laws and regulations that keep pace with electronic crime need to be promulgated and applied at the Federal and State levels.

The pace of technology is so rapid that legislators cannot keep abreast of the changes. No sooner is a new technology announced and introduced for legitimate use then it becomes available for the commission of a crime as well. As a result, laws and regulations fall behind, and the criminal justice system must play catchup to deal with the new crimes and state-of-the-art electronic methods used by offenders. One solution suggested by participants in this study would be for State and local governments to adopt the provisions stipulated in Federal laws and their amendments.

In many States, legislators meet only several months per year. Thus, it is difficult for State laws to keep pace with rapidly changing technology and the criminal implications for society. Often, electronic crimes outpace legislation, such as with the latest trends in cyberstalking and hate e-mail. Model legislation is needed for adoption on a national basis.

The disparity in penal codes among States impedes interstate pursuit of offenders. This is a major issue with electronic crime because it almost always operates outside discrete physical and jurisdictional boundaries. For example, State investigators working an electronic child pornography case in which the crime is a felony will encounter roadblocks in getting the offender extradited if the offender lives in a State that defines child pornography as a misdemeanor. This type of situation is not an uncommon occurrence; investigators are routinely hampered in developing a case for prosecution by vastly different statutes.

Critical need 6: Cooperation with the high-tech industry

Perhaps more often than with most other crimes, the involvement of industry is essential to the successful containment of electronic crime. Crime solvers need full support and cooperation to control electronic crime.

Private industry can assist by reporting incidents of electronic crime committed against them, helping to sponsor training, joining task forces, and sharing equipment and expertise for the examination of electronic evidence. Michael A. Vatis, Director of the National Infrastructure Protection Center, FBI headquarters, Washington, D.C., observed:

> This year's CSI/FBI study confirms the need for industry and government to work together to address the growing problem of computer intrusions and cybercrime generally. Only by sharing information about incidents, and threats, and exploited vulnerabilities can we begin to stem the rising tide of illegal activity on networks and protect our Nation's critical infrastructure from destructive cyberattacks.[1]

Many firms have their own information security units that detect and investigate electronic crime. For reasons involving public image, stock value, and so forth, these incidents frequently are not reported. This limits law enforcement's ability to track offenders' modus operandi and document and prosecute them. Also significant is the lack of exchange of technical information between law enforcement and experts in private industry. Increased cooperation between industry and government provides the best opportunity to control electronic crime and protect the Nation's critical infrastructures from electronic attack.

Some companies are creating innovative solutions to meeting the needs of local crimefighting agencies. In Austin, Texas, a community-based support group for law enforcement has been established. The foundation contributes money and physical goods to the police department to augment their information technology budget. This has proven to be especially beneficial in obtaining necessary equipment and software on a priority basis. When items are needed and can be justified, they are purchased immediately with cash made available from the fund. The foundation also accepts donations of equipment from industry.

Critical need 7: Special research and publications

Investigators, forensic laboratory specialists, and prosecutors need a comprehensive directory of electronic crime training. They also stipulated the need for a directory of resources to help them combat electronic crime.

The Federal Government, State governments, colleges and universities, trade associations, and private industry are responding to the need for diverse training in the field of electronic crime. It is critical to publicize the availability of training and professional seminars if these offerings are to be used to their maximum advantage. A training directory citing current sources of electronic crime training (produced in both hardcopy and electronic versions) would be extremely valuable. The directory should identify the following information:

- Name and address of organization.
- Course profile.
- Level of difficulty.
- Location, dates, and times of course.
- Cost.
- Prerequisites for enrollment.
- Credit toward certification or degree.

State and local law enforcement agencies also are asking for a comprehensive directory of national and State experts and resources. A "who's who" of electronic crime investigators, unit managers, prosecutors, and expert witnesses, as well as listings of laboratories and equipment suppliers, would be a well-received guidebook for practitioners who frequently noted the need for information on how to contact their colleagues in other communities. Much can be learned about the nuances in investigations and case preparation from others who have handled similar crimes. Sometimes, the most valuable information is what to avoid or has proved unsuccessful. This information can save law enforcement personnel time and effort and lead to better case outcomes.

Many investigators and prosecutors are calling for a clearinghouse of information and technical guidance. One such successful nationwide law enforcement network is the FBI's Law Enforcement Online (LEO). However, many law enforcement officers need access to broader information than what is contained on LEO, including access to private-sector specialists and technical data. It is believed that a multilevel secure network would address this need. FBI Agent Steven McFall, one of the study's subject matter experts, suggests establishing a network of computer forensic examiners. This network would link all Federal and State computer forensic laboratories and would promote the sharing of technical expertise, training, and solutions to technical problems in the complex and fast-paced computer forensics field.

Critical need 8: Management awareness and support

Senior law enforcement managers and elected officials need to be more aware of the growth of electronic crime and its impact on their communities.

Many participants and facilitators expressed concern that senior managers do not fully understand the impact of electronic crime and the level of expertise and tools needed to investigate and prepare successful cases for prosecution. It is often the case that managers:

- Do not realize the impact of Internet and electronic crime in their jurisdiction or in society in general.

- Lack statistical data on electronic crime.

- Have insufficient funding and personnel resources to create electronic crime units.

- Are unconvinced that electronic crime deserves much attention.

Police chiefs and managers who are willing to support an investigative capability for electronic crime often must do so at the expense of other units or assign dual investigation responsibilities to personnel.

Managers need data to justify new programs and personnel assignments. However, no reporting mechanism is in place to allow the collection and analysis of electronic crime incidence data, other than the one question in NIBRS. The lack of viable information is a real problem, and better statistics and case histories are urgently needed to capture the true nature of the problem. With numbers, cost figures, and impact data in hand, management then would have the information needed to justify the allocation of personnel and resources.

Critical need 9: Investigative and forensic tools

There is a significant and immediate need for up-to-date technological tools and equipment for State and local law enforcement agencies to conduct electronic crime investigations.

Most electronic crime cases cannot be thoroughly investigated and developed without the benefit of higher end computer technology. Computer systems, software, hardware, intrusion detection tools, decryption technology, and other forensic equipment are expensive and beyond the budgets of most local law enforcement agencies. Even when special equipment is available, it is frequently out of date or unusable in forensic investigations. Insufficient data storage capacity to properly copy and analyze evidence also is a common problem.

For most agencies, a limited number of personnel are assigned to computer crime investigations. Unfortunately, these cases often require lengthy investigations, made even more difficult if the investigator has only a 120-MHz system equipped with a 2- or 4-GB drive, but is pursuing a case involving a 450-MHz system with a 12-GB drive. Cumbersome acquisition policies and procedures also hamper investigators and forensic specialists in their quest for better equipment. Lengthy specifications and bid requirements can delay equipment purchases for 6 months or more. Physical space for a forensic laboratory or computer workstation to conduct investigations is a pressing need in many agencies as well. For these reasons, regional computer forensic laboratories with private-sector support are growing in number.

Critical need 10: Structuring a computer crime unit

As communities begin to address electronic crime, they grapple with how best to structure a computer (or electronic) crime unit that will both investigate crimes involving computers and analyze electronic evidence.

Where does the electronic crime unit belong? Who should be a part of the unit? How should the duties of investigation and the duties of forensic analysis be separated, if at all? The experts are divided on these questions, especially over the issue of whether it is better to staff computer forensic laboratories with specially trained investigators or civilian systems technicians.

On one side of the argument is the contention that nonsworn information technology employees bring a greater depth of technical training and knowledge to the table. Their backgrounds in the sciences, math algorithms, and formula-based problem solving are critical to the forensic examination of electronic evidence. Others note that expertise in investigating crime is the more important skill and

that good training can fill the gap on the evidence analysis side to cover most of the types of forensics local units can be expected to handle. They point out that in any case, a State or local unit rarely will have at its disposal someone who can crack high-end encryption, much less master various computer languages, because it is not feasible to hire one person for each language. According to FBI Agent McFall:

> The blurring of the line between the investigative responsibilities and the forensic analysis of evidence leads to many operational and training problems by making the responsibilities of an employee too broad.

State and local law enforcement agencies would be provided a valuable service if research was undertaken on the issues that arise when police agencies begin to establish better electronic crime investigation capabilities. The experience of successful, existing units should be thoroughly documented along with measures of impact related to different staffing configurations. Results of such research should be widely distributed and considered to be a necessary part of direct technical assistance that is provided to State and local agencies.

Note

1. Computer Security Institute, "Cyber attacks rise from outside and inside corporations; Dramatic increase in reports to law enforcement," March 5, 1999, press release, retrieved December 5, 2000, from the World Wide Web: http://gocsi.com/prelea990301.htm.

Appendix A: Participating State and Local Agencies

State	City	Organization	Participant
AK	Fairbanks	University of Alaska, Fairbanks Police Department	Mark Poeschel
AL	Montgomery	Alabama Bureau of Investigation, Criminal Information Center	George Ireland
AL	Tuscumbia	Colbert County Sheriff's Office	Jimmy Collier
AR	Little Rock	Little Rock Police Department	Clement Papineau
AZ	Phoenix	Arizona Department of Public Safety	David Arnett
AZ	Phoenix	Arizona Securities Division	Phillip Hofling
AZ	Tucson	Pima County Sheriff's Department	Kathleen Brennan
CA	Anaheim	Anaheim Police Department	Mel Vyborney
CA	Anaheim	California Department of Motor Vehicles Investigations	Jack Somers
CA	Irvine	Irvine Police Department	Ron Carr
CA	Long Beach	Long Beach Police Department	Howard Williamson
CA	Los Angeles	Los Angeles Police Department	Terry Willis
CA	Sacramento	Sacramento County Sheriff's Department	Jan Hoganson
CA	San Bernardino	San Bernardino County Sheriff's Department	Timothy Miller
CA	San Diego	California Highway Patrol, Investigative Services Unit	Robert Petrackek
CA	San Diego	San Diego County District Attorney's Office, Computer Crimes Unit	David Decker
CA	San Diego	San Diego Police Department, Fraud Task Force	David Hendron
CA	San Jose	San Jose Police Department	Steve Ronco
CA	Stockton	Stockton Police Department	Tom Morris
CA	Stockton	Stockton Police Department	Henry Freeman
CA	Torrance	Torrance Police Department	Rick Louk
CO	Arvada	Arvada County Police Department	Sandra Fliethman
CO	Denver	Colorado Attorney General's Office	Gary Clyman
CO	Denver	Colorado Attorney General's Office	Marlin Peterson
CO	Denver	Colorado Attorney General's Office	Don Quick
CO	Denver	Colorado Bureau of Investigation	Charles Davis
CO	Denver	Denver District Attorney's Office	Henry Reeve
CO	Englewood	18th Judicial District Attorney's Office	Jim Peters
CT	Meriden	Connecticut State Police	Andy Russell
CT	Rocky Hill	Office of Chief State's Attorney	John Blawie
CT	Rocky Hill	Office of Chief State's Attorney	Vickramjit Sharma

DE	Dover	Delaware State Police, Special Intelligence Unit	Dan Willey
DE	Dover	Delaware State Police, Special Intelligence Unit	Robert Moses
FL	Ft. Lauderdale	State Attorney's Office	Teresa Beazley Widmer
FL	Miami	Miami-Dade Police Department	Laurrick Ingram
FL	Tallahassee	Florida Department of Law Enforcement	Jeffery Herig
FL	Tampa	State Attorney's Office	Charles Korff
GA	Atlanta	Metropolitan Atlanta Rapid Transit Authority	John Dankel
GA	Decatur	Georgia Bureau of Investigation	Vickie Adams
GA	Smyrna	Smyrna Police Department	Henry Cambron
HI	Honolulu	Honolulu Police Department	Aaron Correia
IA	Davenport	Davenport Police Department	Greg Glandon
IA	Des Moines	Iowa Department of Public Safety, Division of Criminal Investigation	Jerry Brown
ID	Boise	Ada County Sheriff's Office	Lon Anderson
ID	Boise	Boise Police Department	Mike Gibbons
IL	Chicago	Chicago Police Department	Charles Padgurskis
IN	Indianapolis	Indiana State Police	Michael Flynn
IN	Indianapolis	Indianapolis Police Department	Joe Mason
KS	Topeka	Kansas Bureau of Investigation	Kevan Pfeifer
KY	Frankfort	Kentucky State Police	Rick Yetter
KY	Lexington	Lexington Police Department	Harold Cottrell
LA	Baton Rouge	Louisiana Department of Justice	Kathleen Petersen
MA	Brockton	Massachusetts Office of the State Auditor	Paul Daley
MD	Columbia	Maryland State Police	Al Evans
ME	Augusta	Maine State Police	Robert Ducasse
MI	Detroit	U.S. Customs, Computer Forensics Unit (previously was with the Detroit Police Department)	Paul Kelly
MN	St. Paul	Minnesota Department of Commerce	John Edwards
MN	St. Paul	St. Paul Police Department	Brook Schaug
MO	St. Louis	St. Louis Police Department	John Wondracheck
MS	University	University Police Department	Michael Bryant
MT	Billings	Billings Police Department	Tim O'Connell
MT	Billings	Montana Department of Justice, Gambling Control Investigations Bureau	Tom Oberweiser
MT	Bozeman	Montana Criminal Investigations Bureau	Lee Johnson
NC	Charlotte	Charlotte Police Department	Terry Sult
NC	Raleigh	North Carolina State Bureau of Investigation	Michael Smith
ND	Bismarck	North Dakota Bureau of Criminal Investigation, Criminal Division	Jeff White

ND	Fargo	North Dakota Bureau of Criminal Investigation, Criminal Division	John Fugleberg
ND	Mandan	Morton County State's Attorney's Office	Brian Grosinger
NE	Lincoln	Lincoln Police Department	Ed Sexton
NE	Omaha	Omaha Police Department	Tom Maille
NH	Concord	New Hampshire State Police, Department of Safety Division	Nicholas Halais
NH	Keene	Keene Police Department	James McLaughlin
NJ	Mays Landing	Atlantic County Prosecutor's Office	Edward K. Petrini
NJ	Mays Landing	Atlantic County Prosecutor's Office	Mark R. Gage
NJ	Oakhurst	Township of Ocean Police Department	William E. Koch
NM	Albuquerque	Albuquerque Police Department, White Collar Crime Unit	Carl Huguley
NM	Albuquerque	Albuquerque Police Department, White Collar Crime Unit	Tim Byrne
NM	Albuquerque	Bernalillo County District Attorney's Office	Ellen Wadley
NV	Carson City	Nevada Attorney General's Office	Jeanette Supera
NV	Reno	Reno Police Department	Todd Shipley
NY	New York	New York City Police Department, Detective Bureau	James Doyle
NY	Oneida Nation	Oneida Nation Police Department	Ted Palmer
NY	Utica	Oneida County District Attorney's Office	Bill Webber
NY	Utica	Utica Police Department	Michael Hauck
OH	Cincinnati	Hamilton County Sheriff's Office	Dave Ausdenmoore
OH	London	Ohio Bureau of Criminal Identification and Investigation	Jim Hawke
OK	Oklahoma City	Oklahoma City Police Department	Greg Taylor
OK	Oklahoma City	Oklahoma City Police Department	Rick Elder
OK	Stillwater	Oklahoma State Bureau of Investigation	Mark McCoy
OR	Hillsboro	Hillsboro Police Department, High Tech Crime Team	Tom Robinson
OR	Portland	Portland Police Bureau	Steve Russelle
OR	Salem	Oregon State Police, District 2, Criminal Division	Stephen Payne
PA	Philadelphia	Philadelphia Police Department, Internal Investigations	Edward K. Monaghan
PA	Philadelphia	Philadelphia Police Department, Special Operations	William Jeitner
PA	West Hazleton	Pennsylvania State Police	Michael McTavish
RI	North Scituate	Rhode Island State Police	James Lynch
SC	Charleston	Charleston Police Department	David Boylston
SC	Charleston	Charleston Police Department	Robert Flynn
SC	Columbia	South Carolina State Law Enforcement Division	Mark Hugeley
SC	Mt. Pleasant	Mt. Pleasant Police Department	David Geddings

SD	Rapid City	South Dakota Division of Criminal Investigation	Chad Evans
SD	Sioux Falls	Sioux Falls Police Department	Arden Georing
SD	Sioux Falls	Sioux Falls Police Department	Robert Thompson
TN	Nashville	Tennessee Bureau of Investigation	William Benson
TX	Austin	Austin Police Department	Scott Ehlert
TX	Austin	Texas Department of Public Safety	Rick Andrews
TX	Austin	Travis County District Attorney's Office	Randall Joines
TX	Brownsville	Brownsville Police Department	Chris Ortiz
TX	Dallas	Dallas County District Attorney's Office	Brian Flood
TX	Dallas	The University of Texas Police	Larry Coutorie
TX	El Paso	El Paso Police Department, White Collar Crime Unit	David Norman
TX	El Paso	El Paso County Sheriff's Department	Larry Wilkins
UT	Murray	Utah Department of Public Safety, Criminal Investigations Bureau	Daniel Hooper
UT	Provo	Utah County Sheriff's Office	Jeff Robinson
VA	Richmond	Virginia State Police	Mike Monroe
VT	Waterbury	Vermont State Police, Commissioner of Crime Intelligence Unit	Jim Colgen
WA	Bellevue	Bellevue Police Department	Michael Cate
WA	Kent	King County Police Department, Fraud Unit	Brian Palmer
WA	Olympia	Washington State Patrol, Computer Forensics Laboratory	Don Wilbrecht
WA	Olympia	Department of Corrections	Donald Price
WA	Tacoma	Pierce County Prosecutor's Office	Franklin Clark
WI	Madison	Wisconsin Department of Justice, Division of Criminal Investigation	Martin Koch
WI	Milwaukee	Milwaukee Police Department	Richard Porubcan
WV	Fairmont	West Virginia State Police	Chris Casto
WV	Wheeling	Wheeling Police Department	Kevin Gessler
WY	Cheyenne	Wyoming Division of Criminal Investigation	Tim Olsen

Appendix B: Glossary of Terms and Acronyms

Glossary of Terms

Attack. A debilitating action of malicious intent inflicted by one entity on another. An entity might attack a critical infrastructure to destroy or incapacitate it.

Banking and finance. A critical infrastructure characterized by entities (e.g., investment institutions, exchange boards, trading houses, reserve systems) and associated operational organizations, government operations, and support activities that are involved in all manner of monetary transactions, including its storage for saving purposes, its investment for income purposes, its exchange for payment purposes, and its disbursement in the form of loans and other financial instruments.

Critical infrastructure. An infrastructure that is so vital, its incapacitation or destruction would have a debilitating impact on defense or economic security. Presidential Decision Directive 63 designated eight critical infrastructures: emergency services, electrical power systems, telecommunications, gas and oil, banking and finance, transportation, water supply systems, and continuity of government services.

Cyberterrorism (information systems terrorism). The premeditated, politically motivated attack against information systems, computer programs, and data to deny service or acquire information with the intent to disrupt the political, social, or physical infrastructure of a target resulting in violence against noncombatants. The attacks are perpetrated by subnational groups or clandestine agents who use information warfare tactics to achieve the traditional terrorist goals and objectives of engendering public fear and disorientation through disruption of services and random or massive destruction of life or property.

Cyber Corps. By order of Presidential Decision Directive 63, this program is designed to encourage government agencies to recruit expert-level computer security workers to respond to future computer crises. This program will use existing scholarship and financial assistance programs and examine new scholarship programs to retrain, retain, and recruit computer science students to work in the public sector.

Defense (or national security). The confidence that American lives and personal safety, both at home and abroad, are protected and the United States' sovereignty, political freedom, and independence, with its values, institutions, and territory intact, are maintained.

Electrical power system. A critical infrastructure characterized by generation stations and transmission and distribution networks that create and supply electricity to end users so that end users achieve and maintain nominal functionality, including the transportation and storage of fuel essential to that system.

Electronic crime. Crime that includes but is not limited to fraud, theft, forgery, child pornography or exploitation, stalking, traditional white-collar crimes, privacy violations, illegal drug transactions, espionage, computer intrusions, or other offenses that occur in an electronic environment for the express purpose of economic gain or with the intent of destroying or otherwise inflicting harm on another person or institution.

Emergency services. A critical infrastructure characterized by medical, police, fire, and rescue systems and personnel that are called on when an individual or community is responding to emergencies. These services are typically provided at the State and local levels (county and metropolitan areas). In addition, State and Federal response plans define emergency support functions to assist in response and recovery.

Encryption. The act of encoding text into an unreadable form called ciphertext through a mathematical process. It can be read only by decoding the text with a key that "unlocks" the encoded text.

Entry point. The point of convergence at which a person first accesses a computer system. For example, a hacker accesses a system and uses it as a launch pad to attack another system, making it harder for authorities to trace where the attack first originated. The first system accessed is considered the entry point.

Exit point. The point at which a trace is discovered detailing that a person has stopped accessing one computer and enters another.

Facilitator. For this project, the contract personnel selected and trained to conduct the workshops and one-on-one discussions with the participants in the field.

Gas and oil production, storage, and transportation. A critical infrastructure characterized by the production and holding facilities for natural gas, crude and refined petroleum, and petroleum-derived fuels; the refining and processing facilities for these fuels; and the pipelines, ships, trucks, and rail systems that transport these commodities from their sources to systems that depend on gas and oil in one of their forms.

Information security (or cybersecurity). Actions taken to decrease system risk, specifically in reducing the probability that a threat will succeed in exploiting critical infrastructure vulnerabilities using electronic, radio frequency, or computer-based means.

Information warfare. Action taken to achieve information superiority by compromising adversary information and information systems while leveraging and protecting one's own information and information systems. Offensive information warfare (IW) may be carried out through physical attacks, the use of special technologies, computer intrusion and computer warfare, electronic warfare, psychological operations, and the use of deceptions supported by intelligence collection and analysis. IW attacks generally are carried out to disrupt operations or infrastructures with the intent to implement individual, terrorist, or national objectives.

Infotech Training Working Group. The name of the predecessor project to the National Cybercrime Training Partnership. The informal network was

formed in 1996 under the auspices of the U.S. Department of Justice (DOJ) and was composed of local, State, and Federal agencies.

Infrastructure. The framework of interdependent networks and systems comprising identifiable industries, institutions (including people and procedures), and distribution capabilities that provide a reliable flow of products and services essential to the defense and economic security of the United States, the stable functioning of governments at all levels, and society as a whole.

Law Enforcement Online. Established by the Federal Bureau of Investigation (FBI) to provide law enforcement agencies a secure network and clearinghouse of information available on the Internet.

National Cybercrime Training Partnership. The organization funded in 1998 by DOJ to provide guidance and assistance to local, State, and Federal law enforcement agencies in an effort to ensure that the law enforcement community is properly trained, prepared, and equipped to address electronic and high-technology crime.

National Institute of Justice. A component of the Office of Justice Programs, the National Institute of Justice (NIJ) is the research agency of DOJ. Created by the Omnibus Crime Control and Safe Streets Act of 1968, as amended, NIJ is authorized to support research, evaluation, and demonstration programs; develop technology; and disseminate both national and international information for DOJ.

National Law Enforcement and Corrections Technology Center. The National Law Enforcement and Corrections Technology Center (NLECTC) is a component of NIJ's Office of Science and Technology. NLECTC provides criminal justice (law enforcement, corrections, and the courts) professionals with information on technology, guidelines and standards for these technologies, objective testing data, and science and engineering advice and support to implement these technologies. The NLECTC system is made up of the national center in Rockville, Maryland; four regional centers operating in Rome, New York (Northeastern Region), North Charleston, South Carolina (Southeastern Region), Denver, Colorado (Rocky Mountain Region), and El Segundo,

California (Western Region); and four specialty centers: the Office of Law Enforcement Standards in Gaithersburg, Maryland, the Office of Law Enforcement Technology Commercialization in Wheeling, West Virginia, the National Center for Forensic Science in Orlando, Florida, and the Border Research and Technology Center in San Diego, California.

Offender. In this report, anyone who commits an electronic crime.

President's Commission on Critical Infrastructure Protection. Commission chaired by Robert T. Marsh and appointed by President Clinton in 1996 to study the critical infrastructures that constitute the support systems of the Nation, determine their vulnerabilities, and propose a strategy for protecting them into the future. The Commission's report was published in October 1997.

Presidential Decision Directive 63. Announced by President Clinton in May 1998, Presidential Decision Directive (PDD) 63 sets a goal of a reliable, interconnected, and secure information system infrastructure by 2003 and a significant increase in security to government systems by 2000. It established the National Infrastructure Protection Center at the FBI to warn of and prevent cyberattacks against the Nation's infrastructures. The increase in funding proposed by PDD 63 calls for research and development to safeguard key computer systems, with a focus on developing tools that can identify potential threatening activities within computer networks.

Protocol. For this report, the assessment instrument used to elicit information from participants in the field.

Task force. For this report, formal operational task forces that comprise two or more law enforcement agencies working together to investigate and solve electronic crimes. Forensic and investigative task forces are included in this definition.

Target. The intended victim of an attack.

Technology. Broadly defined, includes processes, systems, models and simulations, hardware, and software.

Telecommunications. A critical infrastructure characterized by computing and telecommunications equipment, software, processes, and the people who support the processing, storage, and transmission of data and information; the processes that—and people who—convert data into information and information into knowledge; and the data and information themselves.

Threat. A foreign or domestic entity possessing both the capability to exploit a critical infrastructure's vulnerabilities and the malicious intent of debilitating defense or economic security.

Transportation. A critical infrastructure characterized by the physical distribution system vital to supporting the national security and economic well-being of the Nation, including the national airspace system, airlines and aircraft, and airports; roads and highways, trucking, and personal vehicles; ports and waterways and the vessels operating thereon; mass transit, both rail and bus; pipelines, including natural gas, petroleum, and other hazardous materials; freight and long-haul passenger rail; and delivery services.

U.S. Department of Justice. The lead Federal agency enforcing U.S. laws and protecting U.S. citizens. DOJ also provides Federal leadership in preventing and controlling crime, seeking just punishment for those guilty of unlawful behavior, administering and enforcing the Nation's immigration laws fairly and effectively, and ensuring fair and impartial administration of justice for all Americans.

Vulnerability. A characteristic of a critical infrastructure's design, implementation, or operation that renders it susceptible to destruction or incapacitation by a threat.

Water supply system. A critical infrastructure characterized by the sources of water, reservoirs and holding facilities; aqueducts and other transport systems; filtration, cleaning, and treatment systems; pipelines; cooling systems; and other delivery mechanisms that provide for domestic and industrial applications, including systems for dealing with water runoff, wastewater, and firefighting.

Acronyms

ASIS	American Society for Industrial Security
BJA	Bureau of Justice Assistance (DOJ)
CART	Computer Analysis Response Team
CCIPS	Computer Crime and Intellectual Property Section (DOJ)
CSI	Computer Security Institute
DOJ	U.S. Department of Justice
FACT	Forensic Association of Computer Technologists
FBI	Federal Bureau of Investigation
FCIC	Federal Computer Investigation Committee
FEMA	Federal Emergency Management Agency
FLETC	Federal Law Enforcement Training Center
HTCIA	High Technology Crime Investigation Association
IACIS	International Association of Computer Investigative Specialists
IACP	International Association of Chiefs of Police
IT	information technology
ITWG	Infotech Training Working Group
IW	information warfare
LEO	Law Enforcement Online
NCTP	National Cybercrime Training Partnership
NIBRS	National Incident-Based Reporting System
NIJ	National Institute of Justice
NIPC	National Infrastructure Protection Center
NLECTC	National Law Enforcement and Corrections Technology Center
NW3C	National White Collar Crime Center (FBI)
OJP	Office of Justice Programs
OSI	Office of Special Investigations, Air Force
PCCIP	President's Commission on Critical Infrastructure Protection
PDD	Presidential Decision Directive
RF	radio frequency
SEARCH	National Consortium for Justice Information and Statistics
SPAWAR	Space and Naval Warfare Systems Command
TVA	Tennessee Valley Authority
UCR	Uniform Crime Reporting Program (FBI)

Appendix C: Contact Information

Ross Ashley
Director
Law Enforcement Technology
ISX Corporation
2000 North 15th Street, Suite 1000
Arlington, VA 22201
703–247–7852; 703–247–7895 (fax)
rashley@isx.com

Kathleen Barch
Deputy Director
Ohio Attorney General's Office
1560 State Route 56 SW
London, OH 43140
740–845–2410
kbarch@ag.state.oh.us

Richard Baker
Electrical and Computer Engineer
U.S. Navy
Space and Naval Warfare Systems Center,
   Charleston
P.O. Box 190022
North Charleston, SC 29419–9022
843–974–4437; 843–974–5099 (fax)
bakerr@spawar.navy.mil

David S. Beaupre
Intelligence Analyst
Bureau of Diplomatic Security
U.S. Department of State
515 22d Street NW (SA–2)
Washington, DC 20037
202–663–2205; 202–663–2485 (fax)
beaupreDS@state.gov

James Cannady
Research Scientist II
Georgia Tech Research Institute
Georgia Institute of Technology
Atlanta, GA 30332–0832
404–894–9730; 404–664–8329 (PCS phone);
404–894–9081 (fax)
james.cannady@gtri.gatech.edu

Wayne Cassaday
U.S. Navy
Space and Naval Warfare Systems Center,
   Charleston
P.O. Box 190022
North Charleston, SC 29419–9022
843–974–5429
cassaday@scra.org

Frank S. Cilluffo
Director
Task Force on Information Operations and
   Information Assurance
Center for Strategic and International Studies
1800 K Street N.W., Suite 400
Washington, DC 20006
202–775–3279
fcilluffo@csis.org

James H. Fetzer III
Security Specialist
U.S. Tennessee Valley Authority Police
400 West Summit Hill Drive (WT 3A–K)
Knoxville, TN 37902–1499
865–632–4010; 865–632–4063 (fax)
jhfetzer@tva.gov

Mary R. Holt
Director
Alabama Department of Forensic Sciences
1001 13th Street, South
Birmingham, AL 35205
205–933–6621; 205–933–8020 (fax)
mholtbh@mindspring.com

David J. Icove, Ph.D., P.E.
Inspector
Operations Support Division
U.S. Tennessee Valley Authority Police
400 West Summit Hill Drive (WT 3D–K)
Knoxville, TN 37902–1401
865–632–2527; 865–632–2473 (fax)
djicove@tva.gov

Thomas Kennedy
Executive Director
Public Safety Technology Center
Center for Technology Commercialization
1400 Computer Drive
Westborough, MA 01581
508–870–0042

Barry Leese
Lieutenant
Computer Crimes Unit
Maryland State Police
7155 Columbia Gateway Drive, Suite C
Columbia, MD 21046
410–290–1620
BLeese@worldnet.att.net

Dan Mares
Mares and Company, LLC
P.O. Box 464429
Lawrenceville, GA 30042–4429
770–237–8870; 770–237–8815 (fax)
dmares@dmares.com

Stephen D. McFall
Special Agent
Federal Bureau of Investigation
710 Locust Street, Suite 600
Knoxville, TN 37902
423–544–0751; 423–544–3590 (fax)
smcfall@fbi.gov

Howard Schmidt
Corporate Security Officer
Microsoft Corporation
1 Microsoft Way
Redmond, WA 98052
425–936–3890
howards@microsoft.com

Raemarie Schmidt
Supervisor of Instructor Development
Computer Crime Section
National White Collar Crime Center
1000 Technology Drive, Suite 2130
Fairmont, WV 26554
304–366–9094; 304–366–9095 (fax)
rschmidt@cybercrime.org

Tommy Sexton
Director
NLECTC–SE
5300 International Boulevard
North Charleston, SC 29418
843–760–4626
tsexton@nlectc-se.org

Hollis Stambaugh
Director
Investigations and Public Safety
TriData Corporation
1000 Wilson Boulevard, 30th Floor
Arlington, VA 22209–2211
703–351–8300; 703–351–8383 (fax)
hstambau@sysplan.com

G. Thomas Steele
Chief Information and Communications Officer
Maryland State Police
1201 Reisterstown Road
Pikesville, MD 21208
301–776–8957
tsteele@erols.com

William Tafoya, Ph.D.
University Professor of Criminal Justice
Governors State University
University Park, IL 60466–0975
708–534–4022; 708–534–7895 (fax)
w-tafoya@govst.edu
bill_tafoya@msn.com

David Vanzant
Supervisory Special Agent
CART Resource Program Manager
FBI Academy
Electronic Research Facility, Room C207
Quantico, VA 22135
703–632–6902
dvanzant@fbi.gov

Wayne P. Williams
6613 22nd Place
Hyattsville, MD 20782–1752
301–422–7479
wpwilli@earthlink.net

Amon Young
Program Manager
National Institute of Justice
810 Seventh Street N.W.
Washington, DC 20531
202–514–4338
younga@ojp.usdoj.gov